GO OUTSIDE!

OVER 130 ACTIVITIES FOR OUTDOOR ADVENTURES

by Nancy Blakey
photographs by Dana Dean Doering

TRICYCLE PRESS

BERKELEY | TORONTO

In memory of my grandmother Marion O. Holt —NB

Thank you to Camp Fire Girls and Boys for the opportunity to earn my first bead in the Adventure Field of Creative Arts and Photography.—DDD

Tricycle Press
a little division of Ten Speed Press
P.O. Box 7123
Berkeley, California 94707
www.tenspeed.com

Design by Toni Tajima
Illustrations by Betsy Stromberg
Typeset in Chaparral, DaddyOSquare, JCBingo, JCBongo, MetaPlus,
   Mini Pics Uprooted, and Zapf Dingbats

Library of Congress Cataloging-in-Publication Data

Blakey, Nancy.
  Go outside! : over 130 activities for outdoor adventures / by Nancy Blakey ; photographs by Dana Dean Doering.
    p. cm.
Includes index.
Summary: Presents outdoor activities and creative projects, organized by the seasons.
  ISBN 1-58246-064-7
  1. Outdoor recreation for children--Juvenile literature. 2. Outdoor education--Juvenile literature. [1. Outdoor recreation. 2. Amusements.]
I. Doering, Dana Dean, ill. II. Title.
  GV191.63 .B59 2002
  796'.083--dc21
                          2001005914

First Tricycle Press printing, 2002

Printed in the U.S.A.
1 2 3 4 5 6 — 06 05 04 03 02

CONTENTS

AUTUMN ADVENTURES / 67

WINTER CELEBRATIONS / 99

ACKNOWLEDGMENTS

We would like to thank all the people who contributed their energy and support to *Go Outside!* Much gratitude goes to our editor Summer Laurie whose guidance and feedback was invaluable. A big thank-you to photographer Joel Sackett for his professional support, and Dana Drake, Kristan Kelly, and the staff at the Panda Lab in Seattle, Washington. This book was indelibly graced with the invisible work of Dennis Doering, George Gerdts, Chris Lourigan, Barbara Chrisman, Abbi Katz, and Jay Trinidad.

We had unstinting support from Kelly Scribner at Island School, Paul Carroll at Hyla Middle School, Hugh Wallenfels at The Montessori Normandy Park Academy, the Kamimura School, and the practice of Child and Family Psychiatric Mental Health Associates.

And most of all we would like to recognize all the kids whose sense of play contributed mightily to this book, including:

Amy Allen, Brooke Beltico, Julian Berlove, Bridger Bissell, the Blakey boys, Nykky Bradbury, Morgan, MacKenzie, Elaine and David Brand, Bridget Butler, Gareth Chesley, Inga Christopherson, Coleen and Kathryn Cleven, Adriana and Elva Cordova, Dylan, Emma, and Maria Cottrell, Hannah Chrichton, Aaryn Darr, the Deveaux family, Joseph Dewey, Elfie, Robin, and Maximilian Diltz, Tyler, Madelyn, and Amanda Dutton, Alyssa Dyke, Beth Evan, Mark Evan, Harry Evans, Mallory and Emily Farrar, Theo Fehsenfeld, the Geisen family, Joylon Gidari, Tessa Griffin, Marina Heppenstall, the Hepper family, Michael Hopkins, Anna Houk, Andrew and Ryan Hunt, Sasha Keys, the King boys, Lizzee and Andrew Klous, Sally Knudsen, Nick Koda, Lacey Konrad, Robert Lee, the Libby family, Jennifer and Joanna Lockrem, Demy Loulias, Yui Maeta and her brothers Seiryu and Seigi, Layne Mathews, Tara MacNulty, Diego Gonzalez-Medina, Mclanie Medina, David Meslang, Alexis Morgan, Kailani Koenig-Muenster, Olivia Neeleman, the Newman-Rudel clan, Peter Nowadnick, Ryan Parham, Enzo Patricio, Jeremy Pauli, Lauren Piloco, Jordin Powers, Jack Reis, Nash Reijnen, Haley R., Chance Roebke, Tasha Rudel, Brad Russell, Carly Sanders, Lucy and Fritz Schlesser, Collin Schulz, Morgan Smith, Alexa Strabuk, Airana Taylor-Stanley, Seth Moyer Stratton, Jackie Sullivan, Bevan Taylor, Claire and Brenton Thomas, Kristine Valdez, Kara Vandagriff, Stephanie W., Rhett Ward, Krista Webb, Constance Wellman, Isabel Williams, Stella Wilson, David Wolfson, and Perry Wooden.

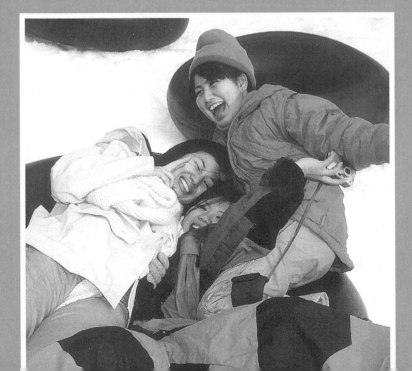

YOUR INVITATION TO ADVENTURE

Welcome to *Go Outside!*

This book is an invitation to a world out your back door filled with ideas and adventure. Once you step outside, the rules seem to change: Your movements can be big and wild. You can be loud and impulsive. You can leap and jump and cartwheel in any direction. All of a sudden no one is telling you to calm down, sit down, or be quiet. When you spend time outside, you are *supposed* to climb and throw and somersault and tumble.

And being outdoors makes you feel very alive as it opens your mind and senses. Some scientists believe we feel this way because our ancestors were hunters and gatherers who needed sharp senses such as hearing and eyesight for their survival. Today we may not need heightened senses to survive in the same way, but when we step outdoors our bodies still recognize the fantastic feeling of being alert and ready for something to happen.

The activities and projects in this book will help guide you outdoors, but don't worry. You don't necessarily need all the materials listed, nor do you have to follow the instructions exactly. All you *need* is yourself and unscheduled time to explore the wild diversity of nature with your mind, body, and all your senses. Use *Go Outside!* to help you make things happen.

THINK GREEN: BE A GOOD ENVIRONMENTALIST

The earth is the only place we have to live, and it is important to make good environmental decisions to help keep our planet green and healthy. When an activity calls for leaves or flowers, try to use the ones that have already dropped to the ground whenever possible. If you must remove them from live plants, pluck from several plants instead of stripping all the leaves from one.

Try to leave no trace of your activity (except snow sculptures, which will eventually melt and leave no trace on their own). Replace any soil you may have disturbed when tugging on a plant. Pick up all litter, even litter that is not yours, including small chunks of plaster of paris, popped balloons, or cast-off pieces of plant. Leave the place of your adventure *better* than the way you found it.

RULES OF THE ROAD

Creativity and adventure sometimes have a risky side. Some of the activities in this book require you to eat wild plants, or cut, cook, or burn something, and it is important to use common sense.

* Always ask an adult to help when an activity involves heat: melting wax, lighting candles, or starting a fire, for example.

* Have an adult help with cutting heavy materials such as plastic soda bottles or whittling with a sharp knife if you are not accustomed to doing it yourself.

* When identifying plants to eat, ask people who are familiar with those growing in your area to help you: people who work at garden nurseries and parks, or local gardeners, for example.

* Never eat any plant or berry that is unfamiliar. Always make a positive identification to make sure it is edible and not poisonous.

* Always wear sunscreen outdoors, even in winter, to protect your skin.

* Wear a life jacket while doing activities in the water unless you are a strong swimmer.

A NOTE TO PARENTS

It was a hot night in August. The weekend had drawn to a close on the heels of a long family hike in the Olympic Mountains near our island home. I was tired. With boundless boy energy our 14-year-old declared he was going to sleep outside that night with his friend and brothers. Turning to me he added, "You should too." I almost didn't hear the words. I was thinking of the spilling backpacks and damp sleeping bags. I was thinking of my comfortable bed and the wonderful book I was reading.

"Because guess what, Mom, tonight is the Perseid meteor shower."

The boy knew I could not resist falling stars, the first snow of the season, or full moons. I smiled. "Well," I said, the fatigue falling away, "I think just maybe I will." We spread blankets and pillows into the sweet sag of an old trampoline and turned our eyes to the heavens.

Every August the earth moves through the leftover debris of the Swift-Tuttle comet. This meteor shower is called the Perseids, and it peaks around the tenth of the month. We cradled our heads in our hands and watched the fat tails of shooting stars arc across the sky in luminous trails of green. A screen door slammed. A seal huffed and snorted in the bay. The air was redolent of basil and saltwater. Each starshot moved the conversation to another idea, another thought. We mulled over the shape of an alien, the size of the universe, the evolution of intelligence. We designed spaceships and pointed out constellations. Wrapping our minds around the concept of infinity, we felt suddenly small and insignificant. On that night all stages of the human cycle—including adolescence and adulthood—joined and were secondary under the wide and wheeling sky.

Thinking back on the past, I find that it is the time spent outdoors, more than any other time, that I've distilled and saved. As we gazed at the sky that summer evening, I felt our busy lives pause while the vault of stars created a night to remember.

Most of us have strong outdoor memories of our childhoods—shooting stars, warm mud between toes, climbing trees or riding bikes for the sheer joy of it. Think of it! Stars and mud and trees and bikes for no reason—not to expand our minds or improve our college applications, but simply because the night was clear or the tree was inviting or our best friend lived a bike ride away.

We live in an age of overbooked schedules. If TV, computers, and piano lessons make up the bulk of our children's lives, there will be little time to create the kind of memories that build a dynamic concept of family and provide a permanent connection to nature. Children cannot love what they have never known. If we, as the adults in charge, do not establish time for unstructured play outdoors, our children will miss the opportunity to stretch their bodies in new ways and discover the out-the-back-door joy of a giddy sled ride on a snowy day, the view from the arms of a tree, or the intoxicating combination of cold water and hot skin on a summer afternoon. These are the small events that shape a childhood and provide a meaningful context to help interpret life as children grow up.

Encourage your children to spend time outdoors. Go outside as a family. Turn off the TV. Unplug the computer. Resist signing your child up for one more lesson or sport, and go outside to an adventure that lasts a lifetime. There are shooting stars out there.

SPRING INVITATIONS

Can you smell the changes in the air? Winter is fading away and plants are beginning to swell and flower. The earth warms and the breeze picks up the scent of green things and wet dirt. Suddenly you are restless and don't know why. Your body is stretching and craving movement of any kind. It's called spring fever and there is one thing that will relieve it: a good dose of outdoor medicine. Fly kites, pick a wild salad, explore your neighborhood, or use this chapter for more ideas to lead you to a cure. The weather in spring can be unpredictable, but don't let a little rain stop you. Your skin is amazingly water-proof, and mud washes off easily. Now go heal yourself.

FLOWER POWER PAPER

This beautiful paper changes color with the flowers you use. You can also press dried flowers or seeds onto the paper before it dries to decorate it even more.

WHAT YOU WILL NEED:

1 cup flowers (any kind will do—roses, buttercups, dandelions, lilacs, etc.)

1 cup white toilet paper torn into small pieces, tightly packed

water

electric blender

colander

vegetable oil

paper towel

screen cut into a 14-inch square (small rolls of screen are available at your hardware store)

newspapers

rolling pin

wax paper

- If the flowers are large, pull the petals from them, and if the flowers are small, leave them whole.

- Place the petals into the blender container along with the shredded toilet paper.

- Fill the container two-thirds full with water, and then blend the mixture on medium speed until everything is mushy. This step breaks down the flower fibers with the tissue to make a pulp, or slurry as it is known in the papermaking trade.

- Drain the slurry in the colander for a few moments.

- Before you roll the slurry into paper, lightly oil the screen using the paper towel to spread the oil. This helps the paper come off the screen easily when it is dry.

- Take everything outside where you have room to move, and the water can drain from the slurry without making a mess.

- Set the piece of screen on a thick pad of newspapers, then place the drained mixture onto the screen. Using your fingers, lightly spread the slurry out over the screen into a rectangle approximately 8 by 10 inches.

- Next, tear off a piece of wax paper that is the same size as the screen. Spread the wax paper over the slurry and use the rolling pin to roll the paper out as thin as possible without making holes, changing the newspapers as they get soggy until the pad is fairly dry on the last roll.

- Lift the screen from the newspaper and dry the paper in an airy place for 24 hours.

- When the paper is completely dry, you can trim the edges.

Write a poem or a letter or draw a picture on your beautiful page, or make several pages for a scrapbook of your outdoor adventures.

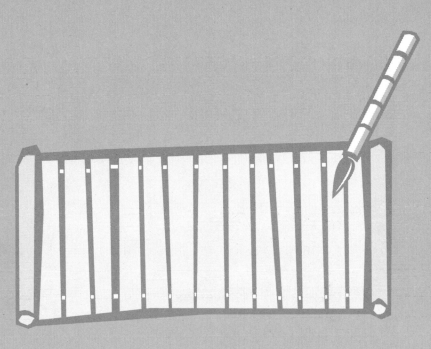

EXPLORE MORE!

The Chinese were the first people to invent paper 2,500 years ago. In the beginning they wrote on split pieces of bamboo that were tied together with string (this is the reason the Chinese write up and down instead of left to right across the page). The bamboo scrolls were difficult to transport and sometimes the string would come loose and the writing would get mixed up. They also used silk cloth to write on, but it was very expensive. The first paper the Chinese made was created from rags that were washed, boiled, and beaten into a pulp. The pulp was then lifted from the water with a screened frame much like the screen you use to create Flower Power Paper. When dried, the pulp became paper.

3

BIRD NEST CYLINDER

Birds cannot resist pulling the soft cotton from this holder for lining their nests, and the white of the cotton makes it easy to track your feathered friends to their nests.

WHAT YOU WILL NEED:

a piece of 1/2-inch hardware cloth
   (1/2-inch wire mesh screen available
   at the hardware store) approximately
   12 by 22 inches

6 feet (approximately) of 16-gauge wire

cotton balls

wire snips

paper and pencil

scissors

- Cut the hardware cloth in quarters with the wire snips to a 6 by 11-inch piece and roll it into a cylinder.

- Using the wire, join the cylinder by weaving the wire in and out of the squares near the edges and tying it off at the end.

- To make a top and bottom for the cylinder, place it on the paper and trace around it with the pencil. Cut out the circle. Use this as a pattern to cut a top and a bottom from the remaining hard cloth. Wire the bottom onto the cylinder and tie it off.

- Fill the cylinder with cotton balls, place the top on it, and wire it into place.

- Make a hanger from extra wire and hang the cylinder where the birds will discover it.

Be patient! It may take a few days.
   Use a bird guide book to identify the birds that visit your nest pickings.

GARDEN BATH SALTS

This project is inspired by an ancient art used to preserve the fragrance of herbs and flowers. For a stronger aroma, add a few drops of essential oil to the sea salt.

WHAT YOU WILL NEED:

fragrant flowers or herbs

a few drops of floral essential oil such as rose, if desired

3 cups sea salt

1-quart jar with a tight-fitting lid

colander

- Take a walk and discover which flowers and herbs smell best in your yard or local park. Mint, lavender, rose, sage, lily-of-the-valley, clover, and honeysuckle all have a wonderful scent.

- Tear the herbs and flowers into medium-size pieces. If you are using essential oil, add a few drops to the sea salt and toss with your hands until mixed.

- Next, place a 1-inch layer of salt into the jar, then add a 1-inch layer of the herbs or flowers.

- Add another 1-inch layer of salt over the herbs and continue to alternate herbs and salt until the jar is filled. Finish with a layer of salt.

- Screw the lid on the jar and set in a cool, dark place until the salt absorbs the smells from the herbs—about 3 weeks.

- Open the jar, strain the herbs from the salt with a colander, and place the salt in a jar with a lid.

When ready to use, pour 1 cup of the salts into your bath.

EXPLORE MORE!

Spring is a good time to:

✖ Plant sunflower seeds in peat pots (you can buy the pot pellets at nurseries or hardware stores). Soak the pots in water to expand them. Keep the pots damp until the second set of leaves appear, then plant the flowers in the garden, placing the whole pot in the dirt, right up to the leaves. Roots will form all along the underground stems.

✖ Make a fort out of a refrigerator box in your backyard. You can get one for free at an appliance store. Paint the box and cut out windows and doors.

✖ Go to your local farmer's market and buy fresh local fruit and vegetables. Make soup or fruit tarts.

✖ Grow potatoes in a tire. Fill an old tire with dirt. Plant potatoes inside. As the plant grows, add a tire and put in more dirt to cover all but the top two layers of leaves. Potatoes will form all along the stems that are covered with dirt. Harvest them in the fall.

✖ Make garden tags for vegetable rows by slipping a cut-out picture of each vegetable in a plastic photo sleeve and taping them to sticks or bamboo skewers.

PASS THE HULA HOOP

This is a good game for mixed company. Adults have a much harder time getting through the hoop than kids!

WHAT YOU WILL NEED:
a group of people

hula hoop

- Line everyone up and hold hands.
- Have the person at the head of the line break hands with her neighbor to place the hula hoop over her arm, then relink her hand.
- Now pass the hula hoop down the line of people without breaking hands!

You can also form teams and race to see which team passes the hula hoop down the line first.

LAP GAME

WHAT YOU WILL NEED:

as many people as you can gather
(start with at least 10)

- Have everyone stand in a circle shoulder to shoulder (it is important to have shoulders touching).
- Next, turn to the right to face each other's back and slowly sit down on the knees of the person behind you.

If you do this right, you will have a circle of people sitting comfortably on the laps of each other. If you do this fast, be sure to sit all at the same instant! If you are really good, try and move the circle backward!

GREENHOUSE EFFECT

Learn how a greenhouse works in a tiny space in your own backyard!

WHAT YOU WILL NEED:
a large, clear jar

- Place the jar upside down over grass or young plants (weeds will work) in your yard and leave it undisturbed for several days.

What happens? The grass inside the jar grows longer and faster than the grass around it. A greenhouse traps moisture from the plants and warmth from the sun as sunlight passes through the glass. Most growing plants need warmth and moisture in order to thrive, and the extra that the plant receives from the jar boosts growth. You can also do this as a controlled experiment: Plant several seeds in identical conditions. After the seeds have sprouted, place a jar over one of the sprouts.

EXPLORE MORE!

You can use the greenhouse effect with dramatic results by growing fruits or vegetables in a bottle. Start when the fruit or vegetable has just formed and is tiny enough to fit into the neck of a clean 2-liter soda bottle (apples, cucumbers, and tomatoes work well). Gently place the fruit inside the bottle while still attached to the mother plant (you may have to strip leaves from the stem to get the fruit past the neck of the bottle). Do not block the opening; the fruit will need a little air circulation. Tie or prop the bottle into place. At the end of the growing season, the fruit will have grown larger than normal inside the bottle because of the greenhouse effect. Snip it off and amaze your friends!

EXPLORE MORE!

On a warm afternoon play different kinds of tag with your friends.

* **STICKER TAG:** The person who is "It" puts a sticker on another player, then that player is "It" and must place the sticker on someone else.
* **STATUES:** Players are frozen into place when tagged, but can be thawed by the touch of any player who is not frozen.
* **THREE-LEGGED TAG:** Teams are made of two people tied together at their ankles and knees with old nylon stockings. One team is "It" and tries to tag another team.
* **SHADOW TAG:** You must have a sunny day for this one. The person who is "It" tags players by stepping on their shadows.
* **FLASHLIGHT TAG:** This is a fun nighttime game! The person who is "It" tags players with a beam of light from a flashlight.

11

WEED SALAD

You don't have to travel to exotic or remote places to find wild edibles. There is a world of eating in your own backyard waiting to be discovered! Many common weeds provide delicious greens for salads, and learning to identify them is a great outdoor skill. Before eating any wild plant, it is important to be aware of the following rules:

✳ **Identify the plant! Many excellent plant identification books are available at the library. Look for books with photographs instead of line drawings. A valuable resource is *Peterson's Field Guide to Edible Wild Plants* by Lee Allen Peterson. There are also people in your community who will be happy to help you identify plants (master gardeners, plant nursery personnel, enthusiastic gardeners, and so on).**

✳ **Do not collect plants along heavily traveled roadsides because of the chemical sprays used to control weeds. For the same reason, do not use plants from your lawn if you have recently applied chemical fertilizers or insecticides.**

✳ ***Never* put an unfamiliar plant or berry in your mouth.**

Half the fun of this project is in identifying the plants! Besides your yard, look for these plants in disturbed areas (construction sites, for example), woodlands, cultivated fields, pastures, and flower beds. Use your plant identification book to discover other wild edibles to add to your salad.

WHAT YOU WILL NEED:

chickweed (also known as crisp sandwort)

dandelion leaves

Lamb's Quarter leaves (young leaves and tops)

plantain leaves (new leaves)

purslane leaves

salad spinner/dish towel

bowl

- Wash the leaves in cool running water or swish in a sink of cool water for a few moments.

- Remove the leaves from the stalks if necessary, and place in a salad spinner, or dry them on a dish towel.

- Tear the leaves into bite-size pieces and place them in a bowl.

- Add regular lettuce if desired, and toss with your favorite dressing.

EXPLORE MORE!

Dandelions were first brought to North America from Europe by the Pilgrims. These early colonists gathered medicinal plants and European food to take with them to the Americas, among them was one of their favorites, the dandelion. Every part of the dandelion is edible. The root can be baked and ground into a type of coffee. The leaves are full of iron and taste best when gathered in cool weather. Even the fluffy seed head can be eaten!

STRING GAME IN THE WOODS

You don't need to be in the woods to do this activity; your backyard can be just as much fun.

WHAT YOU WILL NEED:

ball of string, yarn, or twine

small prize for each player (a certificate for a favor, a small toy, a flashlight for night tag, and so on)

paper and felt-tip marker to make a name tag for each player

- Begin by tying a prize to one end of the string.
- Place the prize in a hiding place in the woods, then unroll the ball of string as you walk around bushes, wind through trees, cross streams, and zigzag your way to the place you will start the journey.
- Tie a name tag to the end.
- Repeat the process for each player.

When you are ready to start, tell everyone to roll up the string as they go along and recycle it for another use.

EXPLORE MORE!

Make a first aid kit for your outdoor adventures. You can place the items in a fanny pack and wear it around your waist, or you can store them in a plastic pouch and keep it handy. The following items are available at a drugstore:

* Ace bandage for minor sprains
* Antibiotic ointment to place on cuts and scrapes
* Bandages to cover cuts and scrapes
* Gauze pads in a variety of sizes
* Needle and tweezers to remove slivers
* Roll of cloth tape
* Alcohol prep pads for cleaning wounds
* Second skin packet (Hydrogel coverings for blisters on your feet or minor burns, also called burn relief dressing or New Skin)

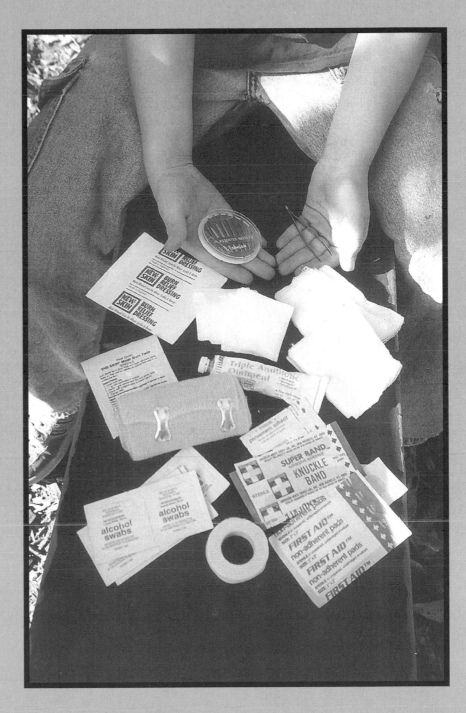

ROCKET BALL

Look for old tennis balls in the bushes near tennis courts, particularly high school courts. You may find more than you know what to do with!

WHAT YOU WILL NEED:

old nylons or legs cut from panty hose

old tennis balls

- Place a tennis ball, in the toe of the nylon. Knot the nylon above the ball to hold it into place. Ready?

- To play with your rocket ball, hold the end of the nylon, swing it over your head, and toss it into the air or against a wall.

To play another fun game, tie on several extra nylons to lengthen the rocket ball. Have one person swing the rocket ball low to the ground in a circle while others jump over it.

EXPLORE MORE!

Celebrate Earth Day April 22nd! This is the day that reminds us to care for the planet we call home. Everyone *can* make a difference, beginning in our own backyards. Recycling newspapers, cardboard, glass bottles, and aluminum cans; composting the organic waste from our tables in a worm bin or a compost pile in the backyard; reusing household items in new ways (like rocket balls!); and reducing the amount of garbage we make every day are real contributions to the environment. Earth Day is a good day to plant a tree, pick up litter in your neighborhood, plan a garden, or sprinkle wildflower seeds along the side of the road. Most towns have Earth Day activities planned. You can check out the Earth Day web site at *www.earthday.net* for planned community activities in your area. Get involved and make a difference!

BALLOON ZOOM

Run the Balloon Zoom in an open space, and add several lines to race different shaped balloons.

WHAT YOU WILL NEED:

oblong balloon

tape

drinking straws

fish line

- Blow up the balloon and hold the end closed with your fingers while a friend tapes a straw to the length of the balloon's surface. Deflate and set aside.

- To make a rail for the zoom, thread the fish line through the straw on the balloon, tie one end to a stationary object such as a fence, tree, or pole and the other end a good distance away.

- Blow up the balloon at one end of the rail, and release it.

What happens? The air rushing out of the balloon will move it along the line. This is an important principle for jet propulsion. Propulsion was first described by Sir Isaac Newton in his Third Law of Motion. This law revolves around the idea that every action has an equal and opposite reaction. In this case, the air rushing out from the balloon backward pushes the balloon forward.

EXPLORE MORE!

Nothing to do? Juggle bubbles! Make a batch of bubble solution by pouring 2 cups cold water, 2 cups clear liquid dish soap (Dawn works great), and $\frac{1}{2}$ cup corn syrup or glycerine (this makes the bubbles last longer) into a jar with a lid. Put the lid on and shake the contents gently to mix. Let it set a few hours before using. Here are some ideas for blowers: try Styrofoam cups with a pencil hole poked into the bottom—dip the drinking end into the solution, then blow through the hole. Try a wire hanger bent into a circle, jar lid rings, plastic berry baskets, and funnels. Put on a pair of cotton gloves and you will be able to juggle the bubbles without them popping!

SKY FLOATERS

Take advantage of spring breezes and make a kite! Fling a parachute out the window! Toss a glider! You can buy high-tech kites and airplanes that fly perfectly, but there is powerful fun in creating your own flying device and launching it on a warm and windy afternoon.

Making these floaters is a great birthday party activity.

WHAT YOU WILL NEED:

plastic shopping bag

string

plastic figure or a nut or bolt to use as a weight

paper punch

paper hole reinforcers or transparent tape (optional)

- Cut open the shopping bag down one side and across the bottom and lay it flat.

- Next, cut a square from the bag (the size does not matter—any medium-sized square will work).

- Now make a hole in each corner of the square with the paper punch and reinforce with paper hole reinforcers or transparent tape if desired.

- Cut four equal lengths of string each approximately 24 inches long. Tie one string to each corner. Then tie the plastic figure or bolt on to the parachute using all four strings (try to keep the strings even in length). If you prefer, you can use small toys or cars as the weight.

- Ready for launching? Hold the bag parachute and weight together in one hand and throw them up into the air. You can also launch your parachute from a window or a tree.

STRAW GLIDER

It only takes three simple ingredients to create a glider. Make several with your friends and see whose goes the farthest.

WHAT YOU WILL NEED:

1 piece 9 by 12-inch construction paper

2 paper clips

plastic straw

scissors

- Cut two strips down the length of the construction paper: one 1 1/2 inches wide and the other 3/4 inch wide.

- Push paper clips into both ends of the straw with the larger end of the clip inside. Try and line up the paper clips.

- Next, fold the 3/4-inch strip in half lengthwise and make a loop by joining the two ends of the paper. Place the loop into a paper clip. Make a loop with the other strip (*without* folding it in half) and place it in the paper clip at the other end. Adjust the paper clips so they are perfectly aligned. You now have two loops on both ends of the straw.

- Hold the glider in the middle of the straw with the loops hanging down, small loop forward. Launch it in the air. If it doesn't glide right, make the larger loop smaller by pulling the end of the strip from the inside. Keep adjusting until you get a good glide!

EXPLORE MORE!

Spring traditionally has some of the biggest winds of the year. Winds are formed when air moves from an area of high pressure into an area of low pressure. Temperatures, too, play an important role. As air is warmed by the sun in spring, it is pushed upward by denser cool air moving in under it. This movement of air creates wind. In the spring, the air over some areas warms up more quickly while other areas stay much cooler. These pockets of bigger temperature differences mean bigger movements of air, or bigger winds. Perfect for flying a kite!

UNCLE JONATHON'S EASIEST KITE EVER

This is a simple kite that truly flies. It is a gem. Thank you, Jonathon of the Big Wind Kite Factory in Molokai, Hawaii!

WHAT YOU WILL NEED:

1 sheet of 8 ¹/₂ by 11-inch typing paper

paints, crayons, and felt-tip markers

1 8-inch bamboo skewer

masking tape (or clear adhesive tape)

plastic shopping bag for the tail

ruler

string to fly with

paper punch (optional)

- Decorate both sides of the paper with paints, crayons, or felt-tip markers.

- Fold the paper in half to 8 ¹/₂ by 5 ¹/₂ inches (strong crease lines make a difference!) and run the edge of a ruler along the crease. Unfold the paper and measure 1 ¹/₂ inches to the right of the crease at the top edge of the paper and make a mark.

- Next measure 4 inches to the right of the crease at the bottom edge of the page and make a mark.

- Using the edge of the ruler, line up the two marks and draw a line. This is your fold line.

- Flip the paper over so the line is on the bottom and fold along the line you have just drawn. Repeat these steps for the other side (or you can simply turn the paper over and fold the other side even with the side you have just made).

- Pick up the paper and hold it as if it were a paper airplane (the folded sides are your "wings"). Then lay it down on its back and fold the flap back and forth until it stands upright; this flap is called a keel.

- To make a support for your kite, place the bamboo skewer across the kite between the two widest points. Trim if necessary and tape into place.

- To attach the string, punch a hole in the upright flap (the keel) of your kite about one-third down from the top (not too close to the edge or it might pull out! Reinforce with transparent tape if desired).

- Finally, make a tail by cutting a plastic shopping bag into a 1-inch-wide strip starting at the top of the bag and spiraling the cut down to the bottom of the bag. Tape the bag strips into place at the bottom of the kite on the opposite side of the keel. You will need 6 to 10 feet of tail, depending upon the wind conditions—the windier the day, the longer the tail you will need. Tie kite string securely through the hole on the keel and fly her away!

EXPLORE MORE!

On rainy days:

* **Make a tarp tent. String a rope between trees (or use a clothesline), place the tarp over the rope, then stake out each corner of the tarp with sticks or big nails. You can also use the side of a fence or the house. Use duct tape to tape one side, then stake the other. Make a cup of cocoa and take it into the tent to listen to the rain against the plastic.**

* **Skin is waterproof! Go for a walk. Drink raindrops.**

* **Measure how far away lightning is during a thunderstorm. When you first see a flash of lightning, count *"ONE-one-thousand-TWO-one thousand-THREE-one-thousand . . ."* until you hear the thunder. For each second counted, the lightning is approximately one mile away from you.**

* **Dig rivers and build dams in a sandbox or some other place where there is dirt. Float boats. Make lakes.**

* **Save a raindrop! Half fill a pie plate or shallow pan with flour. Place it out in the rain until you have collected several drops. Bring the pan in and wait several hours for the drops to dry. Pour everything into a colander and shake the loose flour out into the garbage can. The larger rain pellets you see are formed closest to the earth. The smallest fell the farthest to reach the earth.**

RAIN PAINTINGS

Use the rain to create unique paintings. When finished, cut the paintings into cards or tape several of them together and use to wrap a gift.

WHAT YOU WILL NEED:

poster or tempera paints

paintbrushes

watercolor paper (typing paper works too)

* Paint shapes, scenes, or rainbows on the paper with the paint.
* When finished, place the painting outdoors on a rainy day. Then, watch it rain!
* Check your painting after a few minutes. Depending on how hard it is raining, the paint can take up to an hour, even more, to get good drizzle effects.

Experiment!

CENTRIFUGAL FORCE IN A BUCKET

How is it possible not to get wet with a bucket of water upside down over your head? Let this science project amaze you!

WHAT YOU WILL NEED:

plastic bucket

water

- Fill the bucket halfway with water.
- Take the handle and quickly spin the bucket around in a big circle like a ferris wheel.

What happens? There are two separate forces at work here—one force on the bucket, and another on the water. The circular movement of your arm while holding the bucket creates *centripetal force.* Centripetal force keeps the bucket moving in a circle toward the center around which it turns, instead of flying out in space in a straight line.

If you move the bucket fast enough, *centrifugal force* presses the water into the bottom of the bucket that contains it. Centrifugal force causes the water to move away from the center of the circle around which it turns, but it is held in the bucket without spilling.

EXPLORE MORE!

Before weather satellites and computers helped to predict the weather, people often repeated old sayings to help them forecast. Have you heard the saying for the month of March—*In like a lion and out like a lamb*? It means that if the weather is nasty at the beginning of the month, then the end of March will be mild. Farmers used this saying to help them decide when to plant their crops. *The first three days of the year rule the weather for the next three months.* Test this saying in January and see if the first three days of weather match that of January, February, and March. *Red sky at night, sailor's delight. Red sky at morning, sailors take warning.* When the sun sets at night and lights up the horizon with red, it means that the following day will be clear. If the red sky is at dawn when the sun comes up, however, it means that there is a storm coming.

WATER WITCHING

You must try this activity. I was a skeptic until each member of our family separately found the same water pipes over and over in our yard. The materials are inexpensive and it is well worth the shivery fun of discovering the hidden water places. Check the Internet or your local library for more information and background on this fascinating art.

WHAT YOU WILL NEED:

2 24-inch lengths of 4-gauge copper ground wire (available at hardware stores). Ask to have it cut at the store or ask an adult to help you with using bolt cutters.

- To make your divining rods, bend approximately 4 inches of one copper wire end to a 90-degree angle to make a handle. Repeat on the other wire.

- To search for water (or "douse" as it is called), hold a rod in each hand, fairly loosely, at waist level, approximately 8 inches apart. Walk slowly around your home or yard. When you pass over a water pipe the rods will cross and form an "X."

EXPLORE MORE!

The practice of divining for water goes back thousands of years. There is an 8,000-year-old cave painting in North Africa showing a human figure with a divining rod in his hand. Marco Polo, an explorer in the thirteenth century, reported the use of rods or arrows for finding water. No one can really explain why it works. Some people say it is the attraction of metal or wood to water. Others believe the earth's electromagnetic field is disturbed by water, and the disturbance is picked up by the rods. There are those who say the ability to find water with divining rods is in all of us, and all we need to do is *believe*.

SUMMER PLAY

School's out! The days are long and sunny, and the nights are filled with stars. Summer feels glorious—no homework, no school pressure. You wake up smiling and stretch and think of the long days to fill. There may come an afternoon when there isn't much to do, though, when you are looking for *anything* to shake off that itchy, terrible feeling of boredom. That is the best time to make something happen. Begin with a bike or your own pair of legs. Where can they lead you? Or read this chapter for ideas. Stake out a Tarp Tent (remember this one from page 24?) and have a camp out in your backyard with your best friends. Build a campfire in the barbecue and roast your dinner on sticks. Identify constellations at night and make wishes on shooting stars. What are you waiting for? There are adventures out there!

DYES FROM NATURE

Experiment with the following recipe. Try different plants and flowers than those listed. You can also use fruits and vegetables from the grocery store. One of the most gorgeous golden colors we made was from onion skins, so ask your local grocer to save the skins for you. When plucking plants from outside, remember good environmental principles: Do not pick every piece in sight and replace any soil you remove. Also remember to take care when working around boiling liquids and ask an adult to help.

WHAT YOU WILL NEED:

3 tablespoons alum (available at the grocery store or pharmacy)

1 1/2 teaspoons cream of tartar

water

100 percent cotton white t-shirt (the older the better—wash all new t-shirts in hot soapy water)

4 cups coarsely chopped vegetables, fruits (berries in particular), leaves, or flowers (red cabbage for lavender, onion skins for gold/yellow, blueberries and blackberries for purple, sorrel plant for red, marigold flowers for yellow, nettles for yellow, black tea for creamy brown, oak bark, acorns, and galls for brown). *Experiment* with plants found around your yard and roadsides!

2 large pots (to dye the t-shirt; do not use aluminum, it will absorb the dye)

wooden spoon

- Before dyeing, the t-shirt needs to be prepared with a mordant. Mordant is from the Latin word *mordere* meaning "to bite," and refers to any substance used for fixing colors permanently to fabric. In this case we are using alum combined with cream of tartar (which brightens and evens the color).

- To begin, dissolve the alum and the cream of tartar in 1 cup hot water. Next, pour 5 quarts of water in a large pot and stir in the dissolved alum mixture. Heat the water to nearly boiling, then add the t-shirt. Simmer the shirt on low heat for 1 hour.

- In the meantime, make the dye bath. Place the chopped plants in the large pot and add 8 cups of water. Cover the pot and bring to a boil. Lower the heat and simmer for at least 30 minutes or until the dye is a deep color.

- Next, pull the t-shirt from the large pot with a wooden spoon and drain it in the sink. Wring out the shirt when it is cool.

- When the dye is finished simmering, strain it through a colander into a pot or bowl, and then pour the liquid back into the original pot (the plant material makes great compost!).

- Add the t-shirt to the strained dye bath and stir with a wooden spoon. Simmer the t-shirt in the dye over low heat for at least an hour, stirring often to make sure the dye is distributed evenly over the shirt.

- When you are satisfied with the color, pull the shirt from the dye with the wooden spoon and place it into a sink full of cold water. Rinse the shirt until the water runs clear.

- Dry the t-shirt on a clothesline.

Isn't it beautiful? Wash the shirt separately because the dye can bleed onto other clothes. If you want, you can dye the shirt again in a different dye bath for a new color.

EXPLORE MORE!

For centuries people have dyed fabric using plants, minerals, animals, and insects. In ancient times, for example, the color purple was a rare dye made from a mollusk called a trumpet shell. The mollusk secreted a tiny amount of deep purple fluid that was harvested by cracking the shell open and digging out the vein that held the precious color. It is estimated that it would take more than 8,000 trumpet shells to make only one gram of dye, an amount about the size of a vitamin pill! This purple dye was so rare and expensive that only royalty could afford it, which is why the color purple has always been associated with royalty.

EXPLORE MORE!

Solar energy powers the world; we depend on it for heat and light. It keeps plants growing on our planet by allowing them to photosynthesize, a process where plants convert light from the sun into food. The sun also makes the rain we need by causing water to be pulled up in the sky through evaporation. There, the water returns to the earth as rain. It even helped create fossil fuels (coal, oil, and natural gas), which are formed from the remains of dead plants and animals. We use these fuels to power our machines.

But countries have trouble producing enough electricity to meet the needs of their people. As the price of oil soars, and pollution increases, more people are looking at harnessing solar energy as an alternative power source. If we could collect all the sun's energy that landed on the earth in a year, it would be about equal to the energy created from 60 trillion metric tons of oil! Even if we tapped only 1 percent of this solar energy, it would be enough to give the whole world the same level of power that is available in the United States.

SOLAR SYRUP

Make this yummy syrup for pancakes and waffles with the help of the sun!

WHAT YOU WILL NEED:

1 ½ cups berries

1 cup sugar

1 teaspoon lemon juice

table knife to cut large berries

pot

pie/cake pan

plastic wrap

clean jar with a lid

- Wash the fruit, and if you are using big berries, like strawberries, cut them in half.

- Mix all the ingredients together in a pot and let them sit until the berries get juicy, about an hour.

- Next bring the mixture to a boil and let it bubble away for 6 to 8 minutes. Pull it off the heat.

- When the mixture is cool, put it in a pie pan or cake pan and cover with plastic wrap.

- Place in the sun all day. The syrup will continue to thicken in the sun.

- After 5 or 6 hours, bring the syrup indoors, place in a clean jar with a lid, and store in the refrigerator.

CONFETTI PETAL ICE CUBES

These make cool-looking ice cubes to serve in your summer lemonade. Or make them for a birthday party! Ask an adult who knows plants to help you identify what you pick, and be sure to use only flowers and herbs that are edible! If you are not sure if a particular flower is edible, call your county extension service (in the Government pages of the phone book) and ask. Do not use flowers from the store or florist because they may have been sprayed with chemicals or insect sprays.

WHAT YOU WILL NEED:

blossoms or petals from violets, roses, lavender, calendula, pansies, nasturtiums, thyme, mint, or any other edible flower or herb

ice cube tray

water

- Gather the blossoms or petals.
- Fill the ice cube tray halfway with water and place pieces of torn large petals and herbs, or whole small blossoms into each section.
- Freeze until hard, then fill up the sections with more water and freeze again.

EXPLORE MORE!

Summer is a good time to:

* Make ice hands to cool off. Fill latex gloves (the kind doctors wear) with water and tie them closed with rubber bands. Then place them in the freezer. When frozen, pull off the gloves. Float the ice hands in a swimming pool, or run them over your sweaty face.

* Buy a truck or tractor inner tube from a tire dealer (ask if they have used ones). Curl up inside the hole with the inner tube upright and have someone roll you across the grass for a crazy ride. Hang on tight!

* Have a watermelon seed war. Cut a big wedge of watermelon, and when you come across a seed, squeeze it between your thumb and finger at your opponent.

* Make a grass sled out of a large flattened cardboard box. Sit on it, then pull the front of the box over your feet and hold it as someone pushes you down a grassy hill.

* Make body paint by stirring a couple of drops of food coloring into a plastic dish of shaving cream. Make several colors and paint away!

* Plaster cast animal tracks. Pour prepared plaster of paris into any tracks you find. Wait until hardened, then gently lift.

* Have an outdoor birthday party for your dog. Invite a few of his doggy friends over. Play his favorite games of fetch, tossing a stick, frisbee, or chasing a ball. Make a birthday cake by pressing canned dog food into a bowl, then invert on a plate. Decorate with dog biscuits.

EXPLORE MORE!

So you have a fishing rod, bait (or lure) and bobber, *and* you found a good place to fish. Here are three steps to catching the big one:

- ✖ Cast your line out into the water. After you cast, hold the rod halfway between the straight angle of your body and the surface of the water at a 45-degree angle. Wiggle the bait or lure so it will look alive to the fish. Reel it halfway in slowly. Stop. Reel the line in the rest of the way to get the attention of the fish. Cast the line again.

- ✖ Watch for the bobber to bob up and down. When it does, you may have a fish! Tug upward on your line to set the hook.

- ✖ Reel the fish in slowly. Most of the fish that you catch should be released back into the water. To do this, have a pair of needle-nosed pliers in your tackle box. Stoop down, and keeping the fish in the water, grab the hook with the pliers and gently pull it out.

FISH PRINTS

These prints are a fun way to preserve the special fish in your life, and they make great art.

WHAT YOU WILL NEED:

fresh or thawed fish

water-soluble ink in a tube (available at art supply stores)

paper (typing paper or butcher paper is fine; rice paper is best–available at art supply stores)

newspapers

flat dish

brayer (roller to spread ink–available at art supply stores) or a 1-inch sponge tip paintbrush from the hardware store. A small piece of regular sponge will also work.

- Rinse the fish, pat it dry, and lay it on newspapers.

- Squirt some ink in a flat dish and roll the brayer back and forth across it to evenly cover the roller in ink (or use the paintbrush).

- Roll the ink-covered brayer over one side of the fish or spread the ink with the paintbrush until the face-up side is lightly and evenly covered with ink; if you place too much ink on the fish, your print will be smudged and dark. Don't forget to spread out the fins, which sometimes lay flat against the body.

- Gently place the paper over the fish and *lightly* rub the paper with your fingers–remember to rub the top, bottom, and fins of the fish. Peel off the paper and there it is, a beautiful fish print!

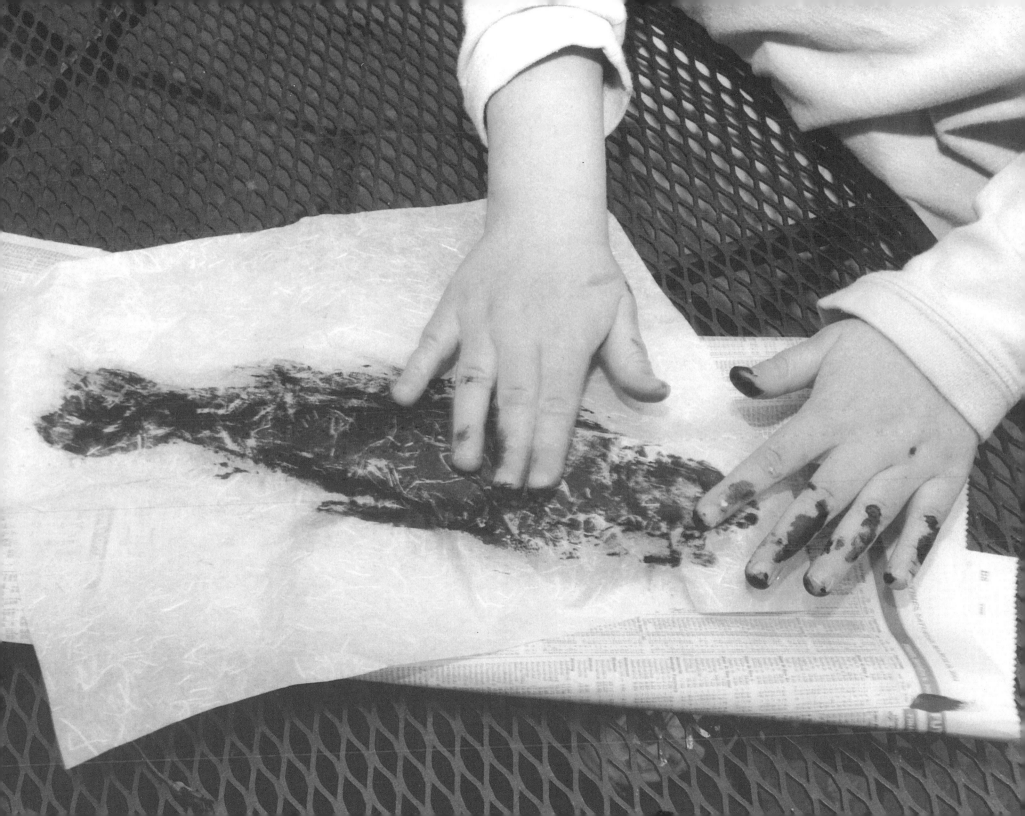

Fish Fossil

This activity is a fun way to permanently preserve any fish you catch, and it is an interesting science project. The process mimics the same chain of events that lead to real fossils—the layers of clay, fish, and plaster represent the earth, organic material, and mud that hardens to rock preserving the shape of the fish as it breaks down.

WHAT YOU WILL NEED:

fish (any type shorter than 12 inches long)

a couple pounds of soft clay* (recipe follows, or you can buy soft clay)

plaster of paris

plastic bag

shoe box

plastic bucket

stirring stick

wax shoe polish in brown or black

- First, you need to freeze the fish whole. Simply place it in a plastic bag and freeze it until solid. While you are waiting for the fish to freeze, make the clay for the fossil:

*SOFT CLAY RECIPE:

3 cups flour

1 1/2 cups salt

6 teaspoons cream of tartar

3 cups water

3 to 4 tablespoons oil

pot

wooden spoon

- Mix the dry ingredients together in a big pot.
- Add the water and oil, and stir until the lumps are worked out.
- Place the mixture over medium heat and stir with a big wooden spoon until the clay thickens and gathers into a big ball.
- Remove from heat and let sit until cool.
- To make your fossil, press the clay evenly into the bottom of the shoe box.
- Remove the frozen fish from the bag and press the fish firmly into the clay (but not so hard that the fish pokes through the clay to the bottom of the box). It should be about half buried. Don't forget to open the fins and tail and press them into the clay.
- Remove the fish and check out the impression. If it is not clear, smooth the clay and press the fish in again.
- Remove the fish.
- Mix the plaster of paris and water in the plastic bucket with the stirring stick according to the directions.
- Pour the prepared plaster into the fish impression until it is covered by an inch of plaster. Set the box aside until the plaster has completely hardened (several hours to overnight).
- Next, tear the box from the plaster, then gently lift the hardened plaster from the clay impression. Now, you are ready to rub some color into your plaster fossil.
- Using your fingers, rub a little of the wax shoe polish onto the fish. Continue to rub the polish over the entire fish fossil until it is lightly covered with color.

You can also make fossils from plants, insects, and shells. You do not need to freeze these to make your impressions, though. Follow the same directions as for the fish.

PORTABLE TIN CAN STOVE

Make your own stove that really works! Keep an extra one handy if your community has frequent power failures.

WHAT YOU WILL NEED:

corrugated cardboard

tunafish tin can (6 or 12 ounce)

pen

paraffin wax (available at the grocery store)

several inches of cotton string or wick

small coffee can

large pan

water

- To make the stove, cut strips of cardboard as wide as the tunafish can is high. You can do this by laying the cardboard beside the can and marking the width with a pen.
- Roll the first cardboard strip tightly, and when you reach the end, overlap another strip over the end of the first and continue rolling. Keep rolling the cardboard strips, one end bumped up against a new end until you have a cardboard spiral wide enough to fill the can. Set it in the can.
- Cut a piece of cotton string or wick 2 inches long and place one end in the center of the rolled cardboard. This is your wick.
- Next, place several chunks of the paraffin wax into the coffee can.
- Now, you will need to make a double boiler–the best way to melt wax because it uses water, which evenly distributes heat, instead of a direct flame, which heats the bottom first.

THE DOUBLE BOILER:

- Pour several inches of water into the large pan, then lower the can with the wax into it.
- Place the pan on the stove and melt the wax over medium-high heat (it can take between 10 and 30 minutes).

- When the wax is melted, pour it into the tunafish can with the rolled cardboard until it is filled. Allow the wax to harden completely.

- When you are ready to use the camp stove, light the wick. Once the whole top is burning, it is ready for cooking.
- To use, hold pan several inches above the flames.

EXPLORE MORE!

It is important to make sure your campfire is safe while it is burning and completely out when you leave. Always keep a shovel and a bucket of water near the fire just in case a spark or coal strays. To put the campfire out when you are finished, pour water very slowly onto the flames. Do not pour in one big rush, or the flames will simply move aside. Pour water until there is no smoke or steam. Stir the coals that are left with a stick and sprinkle on more water. Even when the flames are gone, there may still be hot coals hidden in the ashes that can cause a wild fire. Finally, shovel a layer of sand or dirt on top of the ashes once they are cold.

CAMP COOKING

Next time you have a campfire, try these delicious recipes. There are no dishes so cleanup is a snap!

EGG IN AN ORANGE

WHAT YOU WILL NEED:

1 thick-skinned orange

2 eggs

aluminum foil

- Cut the orange in half and scrape out the fruit down to the white part of the rind (serve the fruit with breakfast).

- Next, pull off a piece of foil big enough to wrap the orange half completely.

- Lay the orange half on the foil, flat side up, break an egg into the orange, and wrap the whole thing up in the foil. Do the same for the other half.

- Place the foil packets in the coals of your campfire (not the flames!) and leave them for 10 minutes or until the eggs are done to your liking.

EGG ON A STICK

WHAT YOU WILL NEED:

egg

salt

pocket knife

stick

- Use the knife to whittle the end of a stick to a point.
- With the tip of the knife, make a small hole at both ends of the egg big enough to barely fit the stick through. A little egg may drip out, but don't worry about it.
- Next, thread the stick all the way through the raw egg and hold it over hot coals or low flames, turning occasionally. In 10 to 15 minutes the egg will be cooked to the consistency of a soft-boiled egg. Hold over the flames longer if you want it cooked a little harder.
- Crack it open, sprinkle some salt, and eat!

MORE! CAMP COOKING

BISCUIT ON A STICK

WHAT YOU WILL NEED:

2 cups flour

3 tablespoons buttermilk powder

1 1/2 teaspoons cream of tartar

1/2 teaspoon baking soda

1 cube of butter or margarine

3/4 cup water

butter

jam

pocket knife

stick

plastic bag

- Place the dry ingredients in a large bowl and mix together.
- Cut the butter into small pieces and add it to the dry mixture.
- Next, using your hands, work the butter and dry ingredients together until the mixture resembles bread crumbs.
- Place the mixture in a zipper-type plastic bag to store and transport it on your hike.
- When at camp, add 3/4 cup water to the bag, zip it closed, and squeeze to mix everything together.
- Pull out a piece of dough the size of a plum and wrap it around the stick in the shape of a hot dog bun.
- Hold over coals, turning frequently until done. Be patient! It will take at least 10 minutes.
- When golden brown, pull it off the stick and serve with butter and jam.

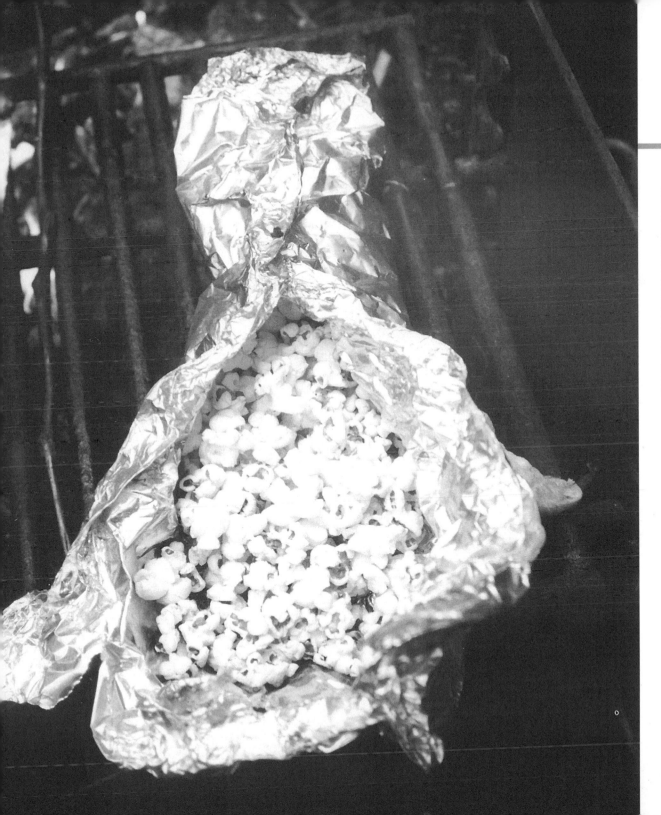

POPCORN IN A PACKET

WHAT YOU WILL NEED:

$1/2$ cup popcorn

$1/3$ cup oil

salt

aluminum foil

- Tear off a big piece of foil.
- Place the popcorn and oil together in the center, and then fold the foil into a big packet around the popcorn, leaving lots of room for it to expand (at least 12 inches long and 6 inches wide).
- Pull up the middle of the packet to make a tent.
- Place the packet into the coals of the fire or on a grate over the fire. When the popping sounds have stopped, open up the packet, taking care not to get burned.
- Add salt and eat!

EXPLORE MORE!

In early August the earth moves through the leftover debris of the Swift-Tuttle comet, making it possible to see hundreds of falling stars at night. This meteor shower is called the Perseids and it peaks August 10th, with more than a hundred falling stars an hour. The meteors begin to flare 90 miles above the surface of the earth, with fat and luminous tails that are easy to spot in the night sky. Keep your eyes toward the northeast, especially after midnight, and watch the best show in town from your own backyard!

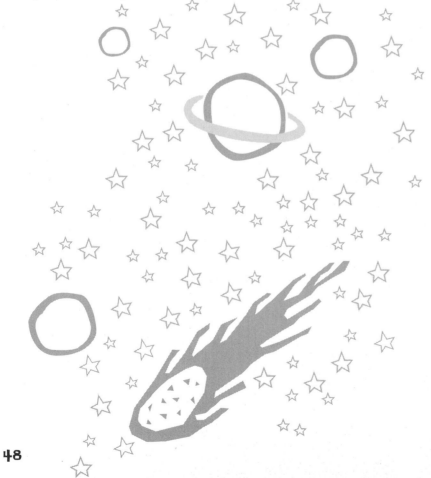

EXPLORE MORE!

Most of the falling stars we see at night are actually tiny pieces of meteors, no bigger than your fingernail, created by star collisions in outer space thousands of years ago. The meteoroid particles were thrown into random orbits around the sun by the collision, and if the orbit takes them into the earth's atmosphere, they burn streaks of light in our night sky as they vaporize in the upper atmosphere. Some of the particles make it through our atmosphere without burning up entirely, and you may pick up a few with the magnet. Meteors can be seen any time of night, but the best viewing is between midnight and dawn. That is when we are facing oncoming outer space as the earth orbits the sun, instead of facing the space we leave behind. Think of driving through a snowstorm at night—you see more snow hitting the front windshield than you do on the back window of the car.

FALLING STAR DUST

The composition of the earth's crust includes meteor particles that have entered our planet's atmosphere every day since its creation, leaving a surprising amount of debris on our planet's surface. It is possible to collect a few of these meteor bits because they are composed of nickel and iron, substances attracted to a magnet.

WHAT YOU WILL NEED:

strong magnet (available at hardware stores)

5 feet of string

magnifying glass

- Closely observe the collected particles with the magnifying glass. About 20 percent of these are meteor pieces.

- The best place to collect Star Dust is at a sandy beach. If you do not live near a beach, try open places where there is exposed ground.

- To gather the meteor pieces, tie one end of the string securely to the magnet, and drag the magnet through the sand or dirt.

CANDLE QUENCH

This game takes a good eye and a true aim! Be sure to ask an adult to help light the candles.

WHAT YOU WILL NEED:

several votive or taper candles per player

box of matches

1 squirt gun filled with water per player

clay or candlesticks to secure candle upright

- Settle a candle firmly in a piece of clay or in a candlestick on a table or rail. Have the player stand a good distance away (how far will depend on the abilities of the players!).

- Light the candle and have the player try and extinguish the flame with the water from the squirt gun.

- Count the number of squirts it takes. The player with the fewest squirts is the winner.

If there are several people with the same score, have a playoff: Take one step back after a successful quench to eliminate players. You may need a new candle for each player, because once the wick gets wet, it is difficult to relight.

EXPLORE MORE!

When you are out and about in the summer, be aware of some of the hazards of the season.

* **TICKS.** These parasites suck their hosts' blood, but the biggest danger comes from a disease ticks carry called Lyme disease. If you find a tick attached to you, you will need to remove it immediately. Use fine-tipped tweezers to grasp the tick's mouth parts as close to the skin as possible; if you grasp only the body, the head can break off in your skin. Pull firmly. You can also spread petroleum jelly over the tick to cut off its air supply. Wait for 30 minutes, then gently pull the tick out with a pair of tweezers. Again, do not jerk or tug because the tick's head could break off in your skin. Another way to remove it is to press the hot end of a blown-out match onto the tick's body, then grab it with tweezers as it withdraws from your skin. If the head breaks off, a physician should remove it!

* **POISON IVY OR POISON OAK.** First of all, know what these plants look like so you can avoid them when you are out tromping around! Identify them in a plant identification book. Remembering the phrase "leaves of three, leave it be" can also help you avoid these hazards. If you come into contact with poison ivy or poison oak, wash the site thoroughly with soap and water, then apply rubbing alcohol on a cotton ball to the area. Don't scratch! The bumps are very itchy, but you will spread them or make them worse with scratching.

* **SUNBURN.** The best cure for sunburn is prevention! Always wear sunscreen when you are outdoors. You can get burned even on cloudy days. If you get sunburned, ease the discomfort by rubbing aloe vera gel on your skin or by taking a cool bath—adding white vinegar to the water will take the sting away. You can take ibuprofin if the sunburn is really uncomfortable.

POOL GAMES

There is nothing like spending time in a swimming pool on a hot summer day, and these games will only add to the fun! Gather the following materials and see where your imagination takes you: balloons, about 10 feet of rope, inner tubes, blocks of ice, 50 differently colored marbles, and votive candles.

BALLOON RACE

This is a race where each swimmer is given the same size and shape balloon to push across the pool with only her nose. First to the finish line wins!

INNER TUBE TUG-OF-WAR

- Tie a rope between the inner tubes of two players. Have each player sit in or hold onto their inner tube.

- Position the players in the center of the pool, and on the count of three, have them try to paddle to the edge of the pool, dragging the other player with them.

- This can also be played in teams. Tie each team's inner tubes together to make one chain of tubes per team. Each team tries to pull the other team across the pool.

BALLOON RACE

52

INNER TUBE TUG-OF-WAR

UNDERWATER TAG

MORE! POOL GAMES

UNDERWATER TAG

Play tag in the swimming pool with the normal rules, except the person who is "It" cannot tag anyone who is completely under-water.

ICE BLOCK RACE

Here's another race across the swimming pool, only this time the participants each have a block of ice in front of them (which floats, of course!). Try to push the ice block across the pool first using either hands or head. You can also make it a relay and divide into teams. Each player waits until her team member pushes the ice to the edge of the pool, then she can race it back to the other side.

DIVING FOR PEARLS

Buy some marbles (pearls) and assign points for each color, making the rare colors worth more.

- Divide into teams and throw the marbles into the pool.

- Everyone jumps in at the same time and retrieves the marbles.

- The team with the most points wins.

FIRE RACE

This game is very fun at night!

- Players each have a lit votive candle held in one hand while they race across the shallow end of the pool.

- The player who reaches the finish line first with a lit candle wins.

Be very careful not to tip the candle and get hot wax on your skin. Scoop any extra hard-ened drips of wax from the pool when the race is finished.

DIVING FOR PEARLS

SUN COMPASS

If you are lost without a compass when the sun is out, remember this activity! Finding north using the sun is most accurate near the summer equinox (June 21st), when the sun rises almost due east and sets almost due west.

WHAT YOU WILL NEED:

1 stick

2 rocks

- On a sunny morning, find an open area and plant the stick upright in the ground where no shadows from trees or structures will cover the stick.
- Place a rock exactly on the end of the shadow of the stick.
- Wait an hour and check the stick again. The shadow will have moved.
- Place another rock at the end of the stick's new shadow.

To find north, put the tip of your left foot on the first rock, and put the tip of your right foot on the second rock. Your body will be facing north.

EXPLORE MORE!

If you are not wearing a watch, your fingers can tell you how many hours of daylight are left! To estimate the hours left before dark, face the sun and extend your arms in front of you. Never stare directly into the sun without eye protection. Bend your wrists in so that your palms face you, and your fingertips are touching. Now move one hand so the bottom of it touches the top of the horizon in the distance (it helps to close one eye). Stack the other hand on top of it to reach the bottom edge of the sun—you may have to separate your fingers if your hand covers the image of the sun. Count the number of fingers it takes to reach the bottom of the sun from the top of the horizon. Each finger width represents approximately 15 minutes.

BEACH CASTING

The beach is a perfect place to sand-cast with plaster of paris. There are several ways you can do this project. You can plaster cast a footprint or handprint, shells and beach glass, or make your own unique mold. Leave no trace! Don't forget to take home and throw away the extra drippings of hardened plaster.

WHAT YOU WILL NEED:

shells, driftwood, and beach glass

sand

plaster of paris (available at hardware stores)

water

stirring stick

small shovel

plastic bucket

old toothbrush

- To sand-cast a hand- or footprint, dig a shallow hole in wet sand and press your foot or hand firmly inside the hole to leave an imprint.

- Pour the amount of water into the bucket that you think would fill your print, then add enough plaster of paris to make a thin batter (about like cake batter–or follow the directions on the box for mixing).

- Stir the water and plaster together with the stirring stick (Note: Saltwater will make the plaster set faster).

- Pour the prepared plaster into your print in the sand–enough to just fill the imprint. The plaster will take anywhere from a few moments to 30 minutes to harden, depending on the temperature of the sand.

- To sand-cast shells, dig a shallow hole and lay shells inside of it, rounded side down, with bits of driftwood and beach glass in a pretty pattern. Pour a couple of inches of the prepared plaster over the shells.

- Lift the cast gently from the sand when completely hard.

You can also make your own mold by digging a shallow depression and shaping the wet sand into a face, animal, shape, letter–use your imagination! Pour the prepared plaster over your creation, allow to harden, then gently lift it. The sand sticks to the plaster creating a natural background, or you can brush most of the sand off with an old toothbrush several hours later when the plaster is completely dry.

EXPLORE MORE!

When you are at the beach, here's how to build the best sand castle:

✖ Use fine sand. Test for the best by getting the sand wet, grabbing a handful, and squeezing it into a ball. Can you toss the sand ball in the air and catch it without it falling apart? Good. This is perfect sand.

✖ Keep the sand really wet as you build. Fill a bucket half full of water and half full of sand. Use this sand soup to build everything.

✖ There are two basic shapes you need to learn for the best sand castle: the wall and the tower. Build walls by shaping bricks with your hands. Stagger the bricks in layers on top of each other until the wall is the height you desire. Build towers by making pancakes with the wet sand. Pile the sand pancakes one on top of the other, getting smaller as you go up so the tower doesn't topple.

✖ Use hand shovels, paint brushes, plastic forks, spoons, and knives for detail work.

KNOTS AND TANGLES

This is a very fun game to play with a group of 10 people or more. At first the knots and tangles will seem impossible to undo, but with a little patience and ingenuity, you can untangle the human knots and get the group back to a circle.

WHAT YOU WILL NEED:

10 or more people

- Stand in a circle, facing center, shoulder to shoulder.

- Stretch both arms into the center of the circle and randomly grab hands of other people. The only two rules are: Do not grab both hands of the same person and do not grab hands with the person next to you.

- Now try and untangle yourselves to create one circle. If it is seemingly impossible, you can loosen your grip and pivot around the hand of another person. Sometimes you may find that, once untangled, you have two separate or interconnected circles! Don't give up!

EXPLORE MORE!

Cool down with your friends on a really hot afternoon with a water war. Fill water balloons, spray bottles, squirt guns, and plastic buckets with water. Make a free zone where a player can be safe and not get wet, but remember, she is not allowed to get anyone else wet from the zone either. Players choose their ammunition, and on the count of three, the battle begins. Every man and woman for themselves!

Another way to cool down is to play wet-sponge tag: Fill a plastic bucket with water and add a large sponge. A player who is hit with the wet sponge is the next "It."

PITCH AND BAT

This device is a good one for learning batting skills without a pitcher! Set it up in your backyard or local park.

WHAT YOU WILL NEED:

clothesline or rope

tennis ball

approximately 5 feet of heavy string

duct tape

bat

- String the clothesline two or three feet above your head between two trees or posts. Make sure they are spaced far enough apart that a swinging bat will not hit them from the midline (you may need an adult's help with this).
- To attach the ball to the rope, first wrap several feet of the heavy string around the tennis ball as tightly as possible from several different directions. Leave approximately 3 feet of string at the end.

- Next, wrap the duct tape over the string and around the ball to secure the string in place.
- Finally, tie the string to the middle of the rope, adjusting the string so the ball hangs at about shoulder level.
- Ready? Swing at the ball with the bat.

EXPLORE MORE!

Did you know that the game of baseball was developed from an old English game called Rounders? Rounders was played much like baseball is today with a player hitting a ball with a bat and then advancing around bases. The biggest difference was the way fielders could get players out. If a runner was off base, the fielders would throw the ball *at* the player. If it hit him, he was out. Early American colonists brought the game of Rounders with them, calling it several different names, including the name "baseball." Eventually the name stuck, and by the 1840s the rules had changed to *tagging* the runner instead of hitting him with the ball, creating the game we know today.

EXPLORE MORE!

The Mountaineers are a nonprofit organization dedicated to the preservation, exploration, and enjoyment of the outdoors. They have made a list of 10 essential pieces of equipment every hiker should have in his or her backpack before going out the door:

- **Map of the area you are hiking**
- **Compass for navigating**
- **Flashlight with spare bulb and extra batteries**
- **Extra food**
- **Sunglasses**
- **Another change of clothes in case you get wet**
- **First aid supplies including sunscreen and insect repellent**
- **Matches in a waterproof container to start an emergency fire if necessary**
- **Fire starter to start an emergency fire if necessary**
- **Pocket knife to prepare food, shave wood to start a fire, and use for first aid**

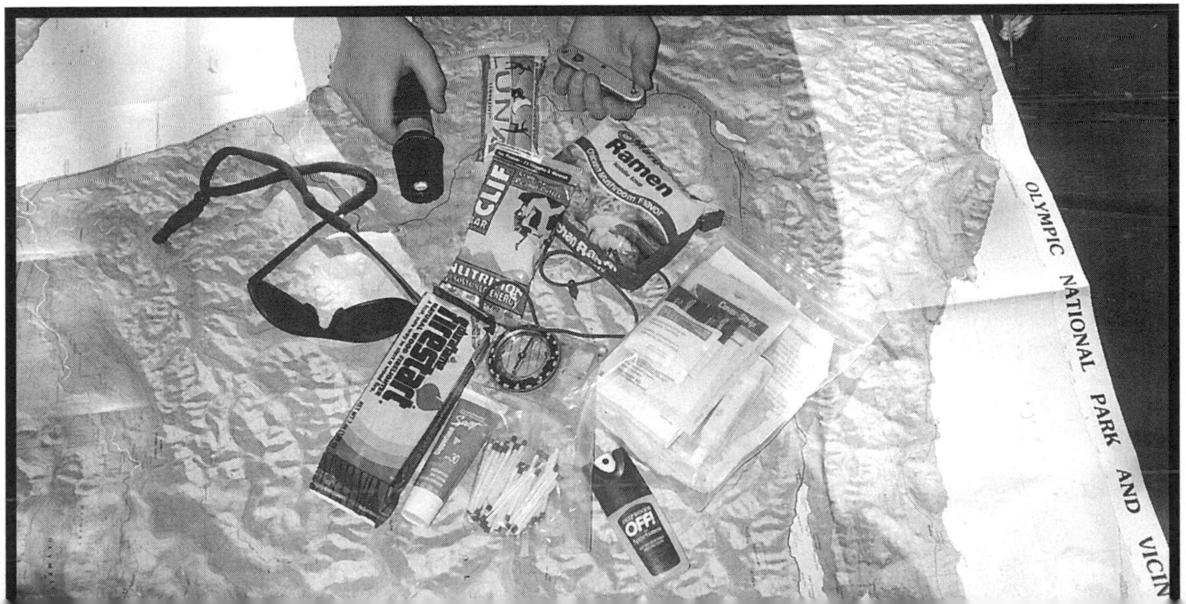

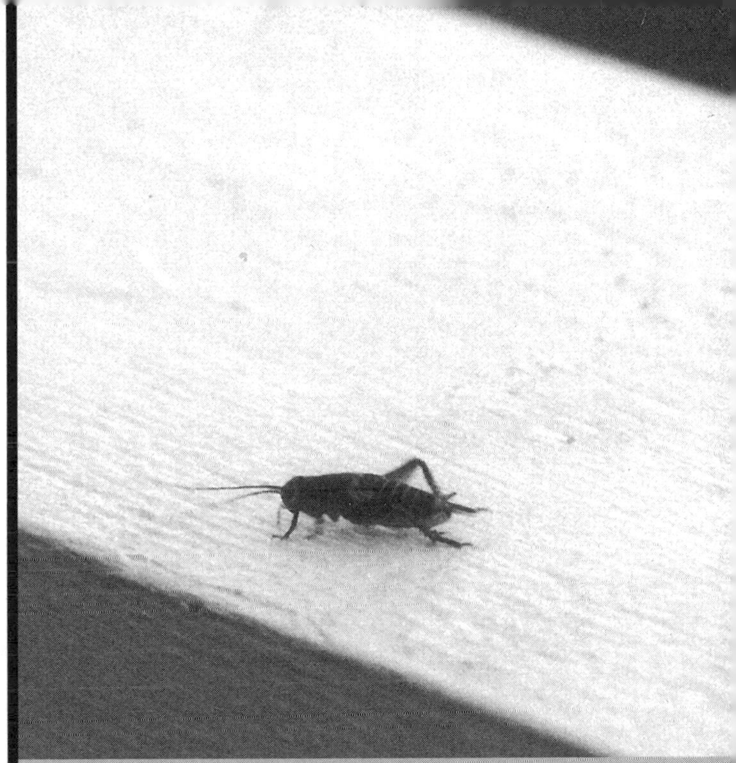

EXPLORE MORE!

Did you know that crickets chirp according to the temperature? The warmer it is, the faster they chirp. You can use this fact to estimate how hot it is outside in Fahrenheit degrees. Using a watch with a second hand, count the number of chirps you can hear in 15 seconds. Add 40 to this number and the answer is the outdoor temperature. For example, if you count 45 chirps in 15 seconds, add 40 and it is about 85 degrees outside.

WATER WHEEL

Water wheels are one of the ways energy can be harnessed. For thousands of years water has been used to drive machines that help people with a wide variety of tasks, from transportation to food preparation.

WHAT YOU WILL NEED:

note card or lightweight cardboard

empty thread spool

glue

pencil, skewer, or knitting needle

- Cut four rectangles from the note card, each about 1 ¹/₂ inches long by 1 inch wide.
- Fold one rectangle in half and glue one half of it on to the spool.
- Repeat with the other three rectangles, spacing them evenly around the spool. You should now have four "blades" attached to your "wheel."
- Run the pencil or skewer through the center of the spool and hold it under running water.

What happens? The force of the water moves the blades, which spins the wheel. This energy can be harnessed by using the water to mechanically move machine parts for turning grindstones, for example, or for making other machinery work.

EXPLORE MORE!

Have you ever been knocked over by a wave at the beach? Then you know the power of moving water. Today, scientists are exploring ways to harness the energy of the sea with power plants that use the movement of the tides and waves to produce electricity. Stephen Salter is an engineer who helped invent a wave-power generator called a Duck. It is a huge flattened cylinder with paddles attached that bob up and down on the sea, looking very much like a duck. As the paddles spin with the movement of the waves, they turn a shaft to make electricity. Salter's Duck converts wave energy to electricity very efficiently, but scientists are having trouble with the mechanical components in the harsh sea environment. If wave-power generators are successful, they will be clustered together in "energy farms" several miles from shore. Eventually these energy farms could produce the same amount of electricity as a large fossil-fuel power station.

WATER BALLOON BOWLING

You can use six or more people for human bowling pins. Don't worry too much about the form of the triangle; it will still be fun even if the group moves around.

WHAT YOU WILL NEED:

7 players

12 round balloons filled with water and tied closed

- Place the "pins" in a triangle: three people in the back, two people in front of them, and one person standing in front of the group of two.

- To play, have the bowler (the seventh player) stand 20 feet away and roll the filled water balloon to the pins. Each player gets two turns, just like in real bowling. Each player gets one point for each pair of feet that get wet. If the balloon breaks and gets everyone's feet wet, that is a "strike"–six points! If the balloon doesn't break, the player receives a score of zero.

- After his turn, the bowler becomes the front person in the triangle, everybody shifts, and a player in the back gets a turn.

Rotate through the players until everyone has a turn. The bowler with the most points wins.

AUTUMN ADVENTURES

Autumn is my favorite time of year. I live in the Northwest where we often have Indian summers–a period of mild days before the cold winter weather arrives. The sun shines softly, without the harshness of summer. The sky is a deep and rich color of blue that fades to the horizon. It is a blissful interval of fair weather to enjoy before the long rainy season of winter. In autumn we fill our days with as much outdoor time as possible–hiking, harvesting apples, fishing, and riding bikes–without the heat of summer or the rains of winter to hamper us. Wherever you live, make time each day to go outdoors and enjoy the extraordinary colors and energy of fall.

SOCK WALK

This activity has several steps, each one interesting to do and connected to the next. Try walking in different places with different socks for a variety of plant seeds.

WHAT YOU WILL NEED:

a long old sock

magnifying glass

potting soil

spray bottle filled with water

9 by 13-inch baking pan

newspapers

- Pull the sock onto your shoe and over your pants.
- Go for a walk in a place with tall overgrown weeds and grass–vacant lots, parks, and roadsides are good places (watch out for ticks if they live in your area).
- Once home, pull off the sock, get out the magnifying glass, and look carefully at the seeds you picked up.

- Next, fill the sock with damp potting soil. Wet the outside of the sock with a fine spray of water and lay it in the baking pan.
- Fold a fat chunk of newspapers into quarters and place under one end of the pan to tip it slightly.
- Leaving the pan tilted up, add enough water so the end of the sock can soak it up until it can absorb no more.
- Put the pan in a warm and sunny place. Over the next 10 days keep the sock fairly damp, but not soaking, by pouring a little water in the pan for the sock to absorb when it dries out. Mist the sock with the spray bottle every other day.

What happens? Plants will grow from the seeds you picked up on the sock (it may take anywhere from a few days to a few weeks for the seeds to sprout). Plants have many different ways of dispersing their seeds; one way is to attach themselves to moving objects, like your socks, in order to cover a wider area to grow.

EXPLORE MORE!

There are many ways a seed travels to plant itself. People, birds, wind, water, and hitchhiking (as in the Sock Walk activity) are a few ways that seeds spread themselves around. The seeds that travel by wind are lightweight and often have wings or parachutes, like maple tree seeds and dandelions. Some of these seeds have been known to travel more than 30 miles on a windy day. The coconut is the largest seed of all; it can float in the sea for thousands of miles before landing on a beach to take root. Birds help to plant seeds, too; Charles Darwin once grew 80 plants from the mud he scraped off a bird's foot!

AUTUMN PLACE MATS

Collect colorful fallen leaves and place them between the pages of a magazine to keep the leaves flat until you are ready to use them. These make beautiful place mats for the holiday table.

WHAT YOU WILL NEED:

wax paper

autumn leaves

iron/ironing board

colored masking tape

- Tear two pieces of wax paper, each approximately 18 inches long. Place one piece on the ironing board and lay a nice arrangement of leaves on top of the paper. Don't place leaves too close to the edge because they will prevent a good seal.

- Next, place the other piece of wax paper on top of your leaf design, and with a hot iron, seal the pieces together with the leaves sandwiched in between. Trim the mat if necessary. To make the mat more sturdy, seal the edges with colored masking tape. You can also make matching coasters if you like.

EXPLORE MORE!

Do you know why leaves change color in the fall? Leaves are green because plants use the sun to make a food called chlorophyll. Chlorophyll is green and spreads throughout the leaves giving them their color. In the fall there is less sun for the plants to use, and they eventually stop making chlorophyll. As the chlorophyll fades away, the true color of the leaf emerges in yellow and orange colors. These colors were in the leaves all summer, but the chlorophyll masked them with green.

Leaves turn red and purple for a different reason. Sugars are trapped in the leaves when temperatures are warm during the day and then drop much cooler at night. The trapped sugars in the leaves turn into anthocyanin pigments, which are red or purple in color.

LEAF CROWN

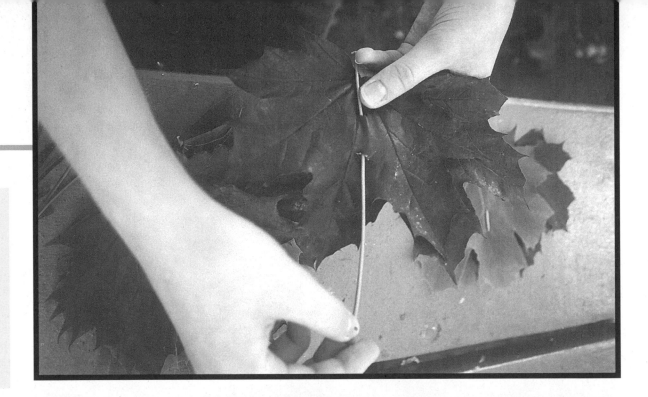

Making leaf crowns and daisy chains were popular pastimes in the pioneer days when children didn't have many toys.

WHAT YOU WILL NEED:

fallen leaves with long stems such as maple

- First, break the stems from the leaves.
- To bind the leaves, overlap two leaves by several inches and, somewhere near the middle of the leaves, push the end of a stem into the two leaves, then push it back up and through $1/2$-inch or so from where you started (using the stem as you would a straight pin).
- Overlap another leaf several inches further onto this set and bind it in the same way. Continue binding leaves together until you have enough to go around your head.
- To make the crown, overlap the two end leaves together and connect them with a stem.

72

OUTDOOR SCAVENGER HUNT

Outdoor scavenger hunts are a great party activity. Use creativity when making your lists by looking closely at what is available outdoors around your neighborhood.

WHAT YOU WILL NEED:

plastic or paper bags for each team, including one with airholes if you intend to collect anything that breathes

1 list of outdoor items for each team (Have them find things like a red leaf, a berry, something that smells good, something pink, a piece of dead wood, a feather, a black rock, an insect, a seed, something straight, round, rough, or sharp.)

- After making your list of items, divide into teams. Give each team the list and the bag to put the items in.

- The team that finds all the objects first wins.

Once the hunt is over, remember to release any live creatures you collected along the way.

SHADOW DANCING

You need a sunny day for this fun way to decorate your sidewalk or driveway with a wonderful mural of dancers! The paint is biodegradable and will wash off cement or asphalt with water.

WHAT YOU WILL NEED:

sponge-tip paintbrushes (or a piece of a regular sponge)

chalk

several batches of Shadow Dancing Paint

- To make Shadow Dancers, have a friend stand in the sun in a dance position.
- Outline her shadow on the ground with chalk.
- Next, paint inside the shadow using a sponge-tip paintbrush.
- Add confetti-like splats of paint in the background around the dancer. Make several dancers the same way.

TO MAKE SHADOW DANCING PAINT:

³/₄ cup warm water

1 cup powdered milk

¹/₄ teaspoon paste food coloring, several colors

small jar with lid

- Mix warm water, powdered milk, and paste food coloring (you can use regular food coloring, but paste makes richer colors; they are available in kitchen supply shops) in the jar.
- Shake it all together. Make several colors.

EXPLORE MORE!

Autumn is a good time to:

✹ Make a huge leaf maze by raking paths into fallen leaves.

✹ Make leaf angels the same way you make snow angels. Lay down in fallen leaves and move arms and legs in and out.

✹ Have your family rent or borrow an apple press from your local rental shop and press apples into cider. Invite the neighbors and make it a party!

✹ Make jam from berries that you pick. Boil equal amounts of sugar and fruit for 8 minutes, then place in a jar and store in the refrigerator.

✹ Walk to school. Many Japanese children do not ride school buses—their parents believe walking to and from school is an important way for them to think about what they learned in class that day.

✹ Go for a walk with your family at night with flashlights.

✹ Carve faces in apples. Peel the apple and cut out a nose, eyes, and mouth. Place the head on a chopstick and let it dry for several weeks.

✹ Save the seeds from the flowers in your yard to plant in the spring. Collect mature flowers and allow them to dry in an airy place. Then shake the dried flower heads over a newspaper. Slip the seeds from the newspaper into an empty film canister. Snap on the lid, label, and store until spring when you are ready to plant.

EXPLORE MORE!

Amaze your friends with this balloon trick! Balloons pop with a loud bang, because when pierced, the surface of the balloon tears as the air rushes out. It is possible, however, to pierce a balloon with a needle and not have it pop. Place a small piece of clear tape on a blown-up balloon and press it firmly onto the surface. When you do the trick, hold the balloon with the tape facing you. Ready? Show your friends the needle, then poke it all the way through the tape and balloon. It doesn't pop! The tape holds the surface of the balloon together, preventing the air from rushing out and tearing the balloon.

BALLOON STOMP

The more people you have for this game, the better it is! You can play this barefoot at the very least, or be sure no one is wearing hard shoes that could scrape ankles or mangle toes.

WHAT YOU WILL NEED:

string

1 to 2 balloons for each player

- Cut the string into 20-inch pieces.
- Tie one balloon to the ankle of each player with a string, leaving approximately a foot between ankle and balloon.
- When all the players are ready, yell, "GO!" and try and stomp out the balloons of other players with your feet.

The person with the last intact balloon wins. You can also play this with a balloon tied on to both feet for double the fun!

BLIND MAN HIKE

This activity shows how much we use our sense of sight for orienting ourselves. Make sure your leader is attentive and trustworthy.

WHAT YOU WILL NEED:

rope approximately 15 to 20 feet (a long jump rope works well)

blindfold for each participant

- Space people evenly along the rope and blindfold them (younger kids may want to close their eyes instead of being blindfolded). The leader is not blindfolded.

- Each person holds the rope with one or both hands, then the leader *slowly* pulls the rope and leads everyone around, over, and through various obstacles, calling out instructions such as "Step up" or "Duck under" when necessary.

- Take turns being the leader.

HUMAN PYRAMID

WHAT YOU WILL NEED:

3 or more people

- Begin with the strongest people on their hands and knees, shoulder to shoulder on the bottom. For example, with 10 people use 4 on your bottom row.

- Three people then climb on top of the first four and place a hand and a knee on the back of the person below her (it is most comfortable to place knees on the lower part of the lower back).

- Two people climb on top of these three and lastly, the smallest person climbs to the very top.

Another fun thing you can do is to make a charioteer with one person standing or kneeling on the backs of two strong people.

Assemble several charioteers and race each other, but be careful! It's easy to lose your balance and fall.

WALNUT WISH BOATS

Make a wish on an autumn night with these floating candles! Ask an adult to help you with melting the paraffin and when you are ready to light your boat.

WHAT YOU WILL NEED:

12 walnut shell halves

Play-Doh or clay

2 blocks of paraffin (available in the canning section of the grocery store)

2 crayons to color the wax

18 inches of cotton string (or candle wick from a candle supply store)

small can (a coffee can works great)

large pan

stove

cookie sheet

aluminum foil

spoon

tongs

- The trickiest part of this project is cracking open the walnut shells into undamaged halves. For best results, place a walnut in a nutcracker with the seams aligned with the bars of the cracker (small end of the nut facing in). Press gently. Pick out the meat and any remaining inner shell and save it for making brownies or banana bread.

- Line the cookie sheet with a piece of foil and anchor each walnut shell half onto the cookie sheet with a small piece of clay.

- Place the paraffin blocks into the coffee can.

- Next, you will need to make a double boiler—the best way to melt wax because it uses water instead of direct heat.

THE DOUBLE BOILER:

- Pour several inches of water into the large pan, then lower the can with the wax into it.

- Place the pan on the stove and melt the wax over medium-high heat (it can take between 10 and 30 minutes).

- Just before the paraffin is completely melted, add two crayons of your color choice into the wax (don't forget to take off the labels), stir to dissolve, and remove the can from the pan.

- To make wicks for the wish boats, cut the cotton string or wick into 1 1/2-inch pieces. Then, using the tongs to hold a piece, carefully dip it into the melted paraffin and place it on the cookie sheet. Do this with each piece of wick.

- To make the wish boats, spoon a little melted wax into a walnut shell and allow to cool for a few minutes (a skin may begin to form), then place the wax-dipped string into the center of the shell.

- Hold the string there for a moment to keep it centered until the wax hardens enough to hold the wick by itself. When the wax has cooled, your boat is ready.

On a clear night, light the boat (with an adult's help), make a wish, and launch it out on the water of a pond, lake, bay, ocean, or puddle. You can even use a wading pool for launching; your wish will still come true! Leave no trace! If possible, remove the boat from the water and throw it away.

EXPLORE MORE!

Mushrooms often appear in the fall after the first rain of the season. Shortly after pushing through the ground, they seed themselves with spores that are as fine as dust. You can make a print of the interesting pattern of dropped spores by first cutting the stem from the cap close to the gills. Next, carefully place the mushroom gill-side down on a piece of construction paper. If the gills are dark, use white paper; if they are light, use dark paper. It takes several hours for the spores to drop, so be patient. Leave the mushroom undisturbed for the most effective pattern, then carefully lift it off. To save your spore print, *lightly* spray it with hair spray. And remember never eat a mushroom you have picked; many are poisonous.

SPRAY DYED T-SHIRTS

This activity is surprisingly neat, but wear old clothing while spraying just in case of drips.

WHAT YOU WILL NEED:

cold water dye in a variety of colors (we used Dylon, available at fabric stores)

glass measuring cup you can pour with

2 cups hot water

spray bottles with adjustable nozzles

masking tape

white t-shirts (wash new ones before dyeing)

salt

- Place the packet of dye in the measuring cup with 2 cups of hot water and stir until it is dissolved.

- Next, add 4 tablespoons of salt and the contents of any fixative packet included with the dye.

- Stir together until everything is completely dissolved.

- Pour the prepared dye into the spray bottle. Mix up other colors of dye the same way and place in separate spray bottles.

- Before dyeing the shirts, use the masking tape to create designs or write a name on your shirt. You can also lay the shirt flat on the ground and place leaves, ferns, or flowers on it to create a picture. When you remove the tape, the design or words remain white against the dyed fabric.

- Hang the t-shirts on a clothesline or lay them flat on a lawn or sidewalk. If you want to dye both sides, slip a piece of cardboard inside the shirt to prevent bleeding onto the other side.

- Adjust the nozzle of the spray bottle to a fine spray and begin to dye! Spray it in camouflage colors (brown, black, green) for outdoor adventures. When you are satisfied with the results, allow the shirt to dry, and then remove the tape or leaves if you used them to reveal your wearable art.

- Finally, rinse the finished shirts in cold water until the dye no longer runs. Squeeze out the extra water and dry in the dryer to set the dye. Wash your shirt separately until the dye no longer bleeds.

MAKE YOUR OWN COMPASS

This magnetic device demonstrates the general directions of north and south. Once you know where north is, the other directions are simple to find.

WHAT YOU WILL NEED:

a strong magnet

a needle

thread

- The first step in this project is magnetizing the needle. Place one end of the needle on top of the magnet and leave it for 24 hours. Test to see if it is magnetized after 24 hours by using the magnetized end to pick up another needle or pin (if it is not magnetized, place the needle end back on the magnet for several more hours).

- Tie a length of thread to the center of the needle, moving it along the needle as necessary until it hangs level.

- Walk outdoors and hold the needle by the thread at arm's length. Turn *slowly* in a circle.

What happens? After the kinks and twists are worked out of the thread, the magnetized end of the needle points in the same direction no matter which way you turn your body. The lines of magnetic force from inside the earth run roughly along the lines of the north and south poles. More than a thousand years ago, the Chinese discovered that when you magnetized a piece of metal, it would line up along these lines. You have just made the same device that the ancients used to navigate!

EXPLORE MORE!

Scientists are not sure what makes the earth magnetic, but they currently believe it is linked to the liquid iron in the outer core of the earth. This iron flows in currents and carries electrically charged atoms and molecules. The motion of the charged particles may create the earth's magnetic field. The location of the magnetic poles move around because of the irregular motion of this liquid in the outer core. In 1948 scientists discovered that the magnetic north pole had moved more than 160 miles from its previously recorded location! Scientists have also discovered that the earth's magnetic field reverses direction every 500,000 years. In other words, north becomes south, and south becomes north! But don't worry, the change is gradual and takes between 1,000 and 5,000 years to complete.

DAVE LEEDY'S OUTDOOR SPINNERS

Dave is an inventive guy who thinks like a kid. He and his friends whipped up these visually mesmerizing spinners in a few minutes, and they found that the longer the tape, the more dramatic the spin.

WHAT YOU WILL NEED:

surveyor's tape (plastic tape available at hardware stores)

small piece of wood (2 by 2-inch board) for each spinner

string

scissors

staple gun (adult use recommended)

- Cut several pieces of surveyor's tape into 3- or 4-foot lengths, and then staple one end to the center of the piece of wood.

- Turn the wood over and staple 3 feet of string to the other side.

- Hold the end of the string in your hand and swing the wooden piece in a circle in front of you.

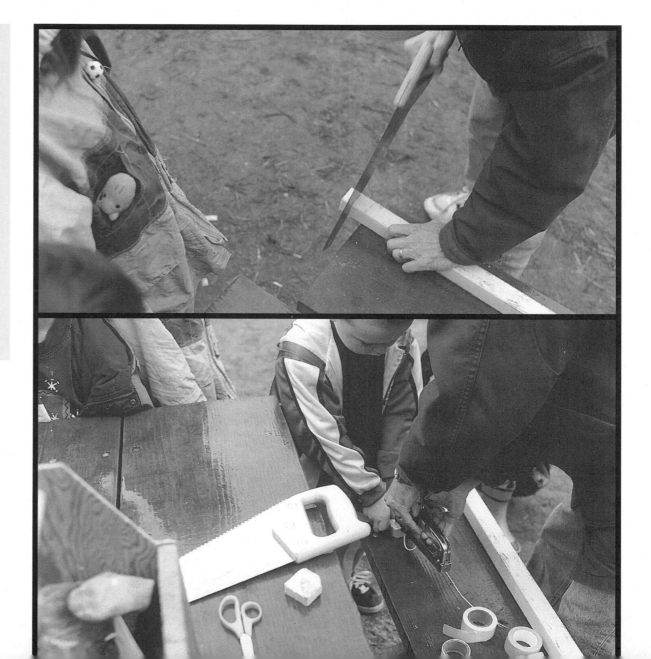

EXPLORE MORE!

Dave Leedy's Outdoor Spinners were inspired by a similar device invented by the Chinese. Dave's idea was to make a spinning toy that was not only fun, but was also simple enough for kids to make and use on their own.

 The process of inventing is the creation of new objects, ideas, or ways of doing things. The man who invented Velcro, George de Mestrel, was inspired by the burrs that stuck to his socks when he walked in the fields looking for damselflies. When he got home, he looked at the burrs under a microscope and discovered that they had sharp teeth that grabbed the tiny loops of thread on his socks. George decided to use this idea for securing things without zippers, hooks, or fasteners, thus inventing Velcro. Another example of the inventing process is to take a problem and solve it in a new way. One girl disliked cleaning the spoon used to scoop out her cat's canned food, so she invented edible spoons that her family could use to dig out the food, then feed to the cat!

 Can you think of a problem around your house you could solve in a new way?

RUBBINGS IN THE CITY

City streets in the autumn are good places to capture the art in objects like manhole covers, building plaques, and tree grates.

WHAT YOU WILL NEED:

butcher paper (or freezer paper)

oil pastels with the paper cover removed (charcoal and crayons work too)

small whisk-type broom

- Take a walk in your city or town and keep a sharp eye out for interesting textures, plaques, or manhole covers.

- When you find one, use the whisk broom to brush small rocks and debris from it.

- Next, lay the paper waxed-side down over the texture or manhole cover, and with the oil pastel held long side down, rub it over the paper until the design appears.

Make a portfolio of different designs from your travels to other cities. You can also make rubbings in cemeteries of your relatives' or ancestors' headstones.

CAN STILTS

Can stilts are a great way to add inches to your height and move in a different way. They also are a good example of making something new and useful from an item that would normally be thrown away.

WHAT YOU WILL NEED:

2 clean, empty cans the same size, opened at one end (tall juice cans work great)

clothesline or thin rope

punch can opener (to make holes)

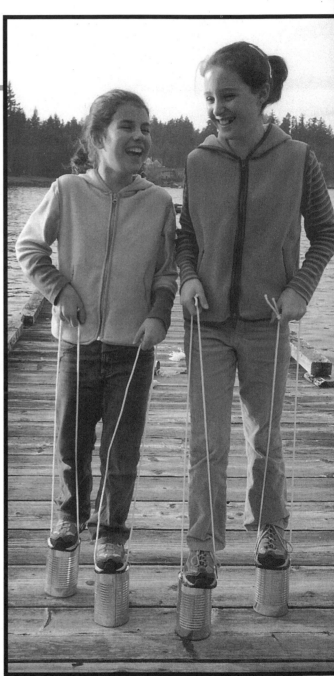

- First, make holes in the cans to thread the clothesline through. To do this, turn the can over so the closed end is up. Use the can opener to make two openings, one each on opposite sides of the can.

- Before you thread the rope through the holes, you need to measure for the correct length of clothesline. Stand with one foot on the clothesline and bring both sides of the line up to your armpits. Mark with your fingers the place where the line reaches your armpit and cut the line there.

- Finally, thread each end of the clothesline through a hole from inside the can and pull up.

- Ready? Stand one foot on each can, wrap your hands around the ends of the line, and pull up to maintain pressure and keep the cans on your feet as you walk.

THREE-LEGGED SOCCER

So, you think you are pretty good at soccer? Well, give this game a try. Three-Legged Soccer requires coordination and cooperation, and is much more difficult than you think!

WHAT YOU WILL NEED:

at least 12 people

old nylons or scarves

soccer ball

- Set up the field for a regular soccer game. You may want to shorten the field depending upon how many people are playing.
- Pick a partner, stand side by side, and use the nylons or old scarves to tie your center legs together at the ankle and again at the upper thigh.
- Divide the sets of people into two teams.
- Play soccer using regular rules.

PUMPKIN TOTEM POLE

These totem poles make a great Halloween decoration in your front yard.

WHAT YOU WILL NEED:

several carved pumpkins

votive candles (one for each pumpkin)

metal fence post

sharp knife

NOTE: Fence posts can be found at local feed stores or hardware stores. Ask if they also have a "slammer" you can borrow–this device drives the post into the ground easily. Some people have used a broomstick instead of a post for the totem pole, but you must be sure the candle is placed away from the wooden handle.

- Decide where you want to place your totem pole and have an adult help you hammer the fence post into the ground all the way up to the crossbar.

- To make the totem pole, ask an adult to help you make a small hole with a sharp knife at the bottom of the biggest pumpkin.

- Slip the pumpkin over the post and place a candle inside.

- Place the rest of the pumpkins from largest to smallest up the totem pole (without their tops), adding candles as you go. You may need to ask an adult to trim the openings a little here and there with a knife to level each pumpkin.

- When dusk arrives, light your pumpkins with an adult's help. Lift the upper pumpkins and, using a long match, light the candles inside.

EXPLORE MORE!

The tradition of making jack-o'-lanterns for Halloween began with an Irish myth. It is said that a man named Stingy Jack outsmarted the devil and convinced him to change into a coin. Stingy Jack put the coin in his pocket next to a silver cross, which prevented the devil from changing back. Jack made the devil promise to leave him alone for one year if he let the devil change back. The devil promised. The next year Jack tricked the devil again and convinced him to climb a tree to pick some fruit. While the devil was up in the tree, Jack carved a cross on the trunk so he couldn't get down without a promise to leave Jack alone for 10 years, which the devil did. Jack died soon after that and God would not let him into heaven because of his trickery with the devil, and the devil was so mad he refused to let him into hell. So Jack's soul was cursed to roam the earth with only a burning coal placed in a carved-out turnip to light his way. Many people said they saw him as he searched for a resting place, and they began to call him Jack o' Lantern, or Jack of the Lantern. On Halloween night, it was believed that spirits like Jack's were especially restless, so people left hideously carved turnips on their doorsteps to scare any spirits away from their homes. And that is why on Halloween we leave jack-o'-lanterns on our porches today!

WINTER CELEBRATIONS

Winter officially begins in the northern hemisphere on December 21st or 22nd, also called the winter solstice. It is the time of year when the north pole is slanted farthest from the sun. The weather is colder in winter, and the days are shorter, but if you dress appropriately, the possibilities for outdoor play are unlimited. When the four walls of your house start to close in and you find yourself short-tempered and fidgety, you may have cabin fever from spending too much time indoors. If you live where there is snow, make up a batch of Kool Snow Paint, or feed the birds seed sandwiches. Gather your friends together and hold your own **Winter Games**. Don't let the weather stop you! Dress warm, keep dry, cover your head, and go outside!

HANDMADE THERMOMETER

This is a simple device made from things found around the house. The results will surprise you!

WHAT YOU WILL NEED:

foil liner from a piece of gum (the kind with paper on one side and foil on the other)

transparent tape

blank notecard

empty spool or film canister

scissors

- Smooth out the foil and cut a strip about $1/2$-inch wide and 3 inches long.

- Cut an arrow-shaped point at one end of the strip.

- Stand the spool on end and tape it to the notecard.

- Next, place a small piece of tape along the bottom edge of the foil side of the strip, then tape the strip in the middle of the spool with the arrow side pointing into the air.

- Place the thermometer outdoors on a cold winter day, or place it in the freezer. When the foil curls to one side, write the word *cold* on that side of the card, and *warm* on the other.

- Now, place the thermometer in a sunny window or in a warm place. The foil strip curls in the opposite direction.

What happens? The molecules in the paper and foil contract at different rates when exposed to cold and heat, causing the strip to bend dramatically.

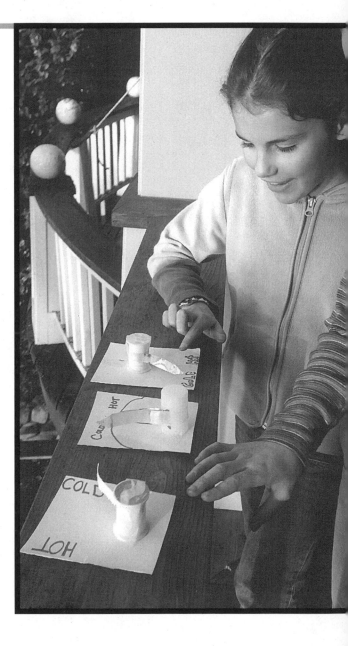

TEMPERATURE EXPERIMENT

This is an interesting project that illustrates the wide variety of temperatures found outdoors at the same time.

WHAT YOU WILL NEED:

3 thermometers (available inexpensively at hardware stores)

small notebook and pencil

- Place the three thermometers in different areas around the yard. If you have snow, place one *into* the snow. Consider placing one in the sun against a wall, one in the shade under a tree, in a puddle of water, dirt, or leafy debris—use your imagination!

- Write down the locations in the notebook and beside each location *hypothesize* (a big word for a logical guess) which places would have the highest and lowest temperatures.

- Leave the thermometers for at least an hour. If you have the time, leave the thermometers for several days, checking them two or three times a day to record the time and temperatures in the notebooks.

What happens? The temperature will vary with each place, depending upon the time of day and the amount of sun or insulation in each location.

EXPLORE MORE!

When the wind blows on a winter day, you feel colder because the layer of warm air around your body is stripped away by the breeze. The faster the wind blows, the faster the body loses heat, and the colder you feel. What is happening is called *windchill*. Two Antarctic explorers in the late 1940s determined a way of figuring out windchill to help people dress warm enough in the winter. This is particularly important in places where winter temperatures drop very low. An example of windchill is when the temperature is 10 degrees Fahrenheit (or around –12 Celcius) and the wind is blowing 10 miles per hour, the windchill effect makes you feel as if it were –9 degrees Fahrenheit (or around –25 Celcius). Quite a difference from the actual temperature! If you have access to the Internet you can check out the windchill formula or link to a windchill table at *www.infoplease.com/ipa/A0001374.html*.

EXPLORE MORE!

Winter is a good time to:

✖ Polish the rocks you collected during the summer in a rock tumbler. These small machines are available at rock shops.

✖ Make snowballs and place them in a zipper-type plastic bag. Place the bag in the freezer to save them for a snowball fight in July.

✖ Blow bubbles outdoors when it is well below freezing. You will make ice bubbles.

✖ Leave different kinds of tracks in the snow for friends to guess how they were made. For example: Hop on one leg, skip, jump, tippy-toe, run, walk, cartwheel, somersault, and so on.

✖ Rent snowshoes and go for a night walk on a full moon.

✖ Build an igloo in the snow using a 5-gallon bucket as a form to make snow "bricks" to build the structure.

PAPER BAG SAND LANTERNS

The soft glow of these lanterns lining a walk is spectacular. These are fun to make before a holiday party.

WHAT YOU WILL NEED:

lunch-size paper bags

sand (available at hardware or lumber stores by the bag)

votive candles

felt-tip markers or tempera paints

- Decorate the outside of the bags with the markers or paints. Next, open the bags and roll down a 3- to 4-inch cuff.

- Place sand several inches deep inside each bag.

- Next, place a votive candle firmly in the center. When you light the candle, make sure that the flame is well away from the sides of the bag!

BACKYARD BIRD CAFÉ

FOOD GARLAND

Invite your feathered friends to your backyard for the best bird fare in town! Most produce departments in grocery stores cull out damaged or overripe fruits and are happy to give them away. Use the following list as a guide for what to collect.

WHAT YOU WILL NEED:

unsalted popcorn

square rice/wheat/corn cereal

cranberries

small chunks of apple, oranges, pears, bananas

baskets

darning needle (larger and have blunter ends than regular needles)

heavy-duty thread

- Place the food in baskets and set them on a table.

- To begin the garland, tie one end of a length of thread 3 to 5 feet long to the eye of the needle. To start, thread the needle through a big piece of sturdy fruit like an apple and knot the thread around it so it can act as an anchor for the rest of the items.

- Next, thread the food items on in any order, leaving enough thread when you are done to tie off the last piece of fruit.

- Hang the garland in a tree, branch, or fence where your family can watch the birds enjoy their feast!

EXPLORE MORE!

If you have a window that birds seem to run into often, hang up strips of Mylar from the top of the window to flutter in the breeze and scare them off. Many birds recover within a few minutes after hitting a window, and it is best to leave them alone. If a bird is stunned and not moving after several minutes, or if you have cats or dogs that could attack it while it is recovering on the ground, you will need to help it. Carefully pick up the bird with a towel and gently place it in a cardboard box. Cover the box with a large towel or blanket and put it somewhere quiet. When the bird begins to stir, take the box outdoors, remove the blanket, and step back until it flies away.

105

MORE! BACKYARD BIRD CAFÉ

PEANUT BUTTER SNACKS

Birds need extra fat in their diet during the winter in order to keep warm, and peanut butter does the trick.

WHAT YOU WILL NEED:

unsalted rice cakes

peanuts

sunflower seeds especially for birds, not the salted ones for humans

pumpkin seeds (optional)

birdseed

peanut butter

newspapers

pencil/string

- Cover your work area with newspapers.
- Place the peanuts, seeds, and birdseed on individual, shallow plates.
- Next, spread the rice cakes with the peanut butter, then add any or all of the other ingredients on top.
- Place outdoors; you can hang these by drilling a hole with a blunt pencil in the rice cake, then threading string through the hole and hanging them from the branch of a tree.

SEED SANDWICHES

Make a picnic with these sandwiches for you and the birds (leave the birdseed out of yours!).

WHAT YOU WILL NEED:

bread slices

peanut butter

honey

birdseed

cookie cutters

pencil/string

- To make your sandwiches, use a cookie cutter to cut a shape from two slices of bread.

- Spread one piece with peanut butter, the other with honey.

- Sprinkle birdseed on both sides of the sandwich and press the two slices, sticky sides together.

- Drill a hole with the pencil near the top of the sandwich, thread the string through the hole, and hang from the branches of a tree.

SODA BOTTLE BIRD FEEDER

Birds love to visit this simple feeder. Remember to keep it filled; birds remember where food is placed and will rely on your generosity when it is scarce.

WHAT YOU WILL NEED:

wire coat hanger

large nail

1-liter plastic soda bottle with cap (emptied and rinsed out)

plastic lid (from a coffee can, large yogurt container, and so on)

birdseed

wire cutters

pliers

small knife

pencil

- Using the wire cutters, remove most of the bottom wire of the clothes hanger, leaving the curves and about 1 inch of wire on both sides.

- To make holes in the bottle for the wire handle, hold the nail with the pliers over an open flame such as a gas stove or lighter (ask an adult to help!) for a few moments, then press the hot nail into the plastic bottle an inch or two from the bottom. Repeat these steps to make a hole on the opposite side.

- Place the curved corners of the hanger into the holes.

- Next, cut three equally spaced tiny triangles, about the size of a kernel of corn, around the neck of the bottle, just where it starts to bulge.

- To make the feeder tray, trace around the bottle cap in the center of the plastic lid.

- Using a small knife, cut out the traced area just *inside* the circle–it is better to cut the circle too small than too large!

- Slip the lid over the mouth of the bottle and settle it evenly.

- Fill the bottle with birdseed, replace the cap, turn the bottle upside down, and hang it where you can watch your visitors. If the triangles seem too large and the seed spills out too quickly, place a small piece of tape over the holes to reduce them in size.

SNOW SLUSHY

Be sure to use only freshly fallen, clean snow for this recipe. You can vary the flavor of the slushy with your choice of juice concentrate.

WHAT YOU WILL NEED:

1 can of frozen juice concentrate
   (defrosted)

large bowl of clean snow

large spoon

- Using a large spoon, stir some of the juice concentrate into the bowl of snow. Taste it.
- Add more concentrate and stir it up until the slushy tastes perfect.
- Spoon into individual cups and serve.
- Keep leftovers (if there are any!) in the freezer.

EXPLORE MORE!

There are no trees in the Arctic. The Inuit people who live there had to be resourceful in order to survive, and when they needed shelter from harsh winter storms, they built igloos from the snow for their homes. To build an igloo all you need are three things: snow, a long knife or saw, and several hours of hard work. The bricks, weighing up to 20 pounds each, must be cut from good solid snow. The bricks are laid side by side in a circle, then more bricks are stacked on top of those, with each layer leaning slightly in toward the center of the circle. The bricks at the top need to be carefully rounded with a sharp knife, while someone inside the igloo helps to place the last brick on top. Then, to get out of the enclosed space, the person who helped place the bricks from the inside cuts a small door out of the side bricks. A chimney is then cut (for the fires they will need to keep warm) and, finally, a window. The windowpane is usually a block of sea ice, cut from the ocean. Today the Inuit live in regular homes, but they continue to build igloos as cozy hunting shelters in the snowy Arctic landscape.

SNOW SCULPTURES

The difference between snowmen and snow sculptures is in the variety of forms and the great detail you can achieve with sculptures. The secret is in the snow–you want it heavy enough for sculpting with small tools. Add water if necessary.

WHAT YOU WILL NEED:

snow

snow shovels

plastic buckets

hand trowels

spoon for fine details

spray bottle of water

- Make a mound of snow larger than your idea.

- As you add snow, pack it down hard with the shovel or stomp on it. If your snow is too dry and does not pack well, add water from a bucket to each layer. The idea is to create snow firm enough to carve details.

You can make anything into a snow sculpture–from creations as elaborate as dragons and castles, to those as simple as a boat or a cat. For something easy like a turtle, use the shovel to pack snow in the general shape of a turtle, compacting the snow down tight, adding water to the layers if necessary. Use the trowel to define the shell: Scoop snow out along the bottom to make the turtle look freestanding. Carve out legs, a tail, the head. Use the spoon to carve out fine details like the pattern on the shell or the eyes. For a glossy finish, mist the turtle lightly with the spray bottle, or you can paint your creation with snow paint (page 115).

For even more fun, ask friends over and hold a snow sculpture festival. When you are finished creating the sculptures, invite the neighborhood over and make it a winter party!

EXPLORE MORE!

Sledding down a snowy hill is a fun way to spend an afternoon. Besides the discs and sleds sold at hardware stores, you can use plastic bags, inner tubes, garbage can lids, and plastic trays for sliding. Before you head to the hills, it is important to remember that fun can quickly turn to tragedy if you are not careful. Always follow these rules for an exciting and safe sledding day:

- ✖ Sled only during daylight hours.

- ✖ Check the hill for rocks, stumps, or obstacles *before* sledding.

- ✖ Wear a bicycle helmet! It is excellent protection against head injuries.

- ✖ Avoid sledding in steep, rocky terrain, and places with trees.

- ✖ Practice stopping: Drag your feet or make a sharp right turn. In an emergency if the sled can't be stopped, roll from it to the ground, letting the sled go on without you.

- ✖ Never sled near roads, parking lots, or bodies of water.

- ✖ Keep your feet and legs on the sledding device as you go down the hill.

KOOL SNOW PAINT

You can use this biodegradable paint on your snow sculptures too!

WHAT YOU WILL NEED:

a spray bottle for each color

water

packets of unsweetened Kool-Aid (use different flavors for different colors)

- Fill a spray bottle with water and add a packet of Kool-Aid.
- Shake until mixed. Mix other colors the same way.
- Using the freshly fallen snow in your yard as a canvas, spray the paint onto it.

Write messages or play tic-tac-toe. Make snow paint Valentine hearts or make a maze. Use your imagination! The paint will fade over time or get covered up by the next snowfall.

EXPLORE MORE!

The constellation Orion the Hunter is one of the brightest constellations in the winter sky in the northern hemisphere. The seven supergiant stars that shape his figure are much larger and more brilliant than the sun, and the constellation dominates the southern sky on a clear winter night. Orion is a hunter by profession, and he is well armed with a shield, a club, and a sword that hangs from his belt. Look for two bright stars at his shoulders, three in a row at his belt, and two at his knees. If you look closely you can see the dimmer stars that make his upright arm holding the club and the shield in his left hand.

Winter is an excellent time to learn constellations. Cold air is usually drier than warm air and less moisture means clearer skies to view the constellations. This season is also when the earth, in its orbit around the sun, faces the richest region of stars in our galaxy. An excellent resource book to help you identify constellations is H. A. Rey's *The Stars: A New Way to See Them.*

SNOW OLYMPICS

Now, you can have your own wacky Winter Games! Make the medals with gold, silver, and bronze spray paint from the hardware store, and spray costume jewelry from garage sales or thrift shops. If you don't get snow where you live, adapt the activities: Use a tennis ball or frisbee for the Hula Target, tree stumps for the Rope Pull, and toss the inner tube, instead of riding it, then measure how long it rolls upright.

SQUASH TOSS

Use an acorn squash for this event.

- Draw a line in the snow or use a rope that the participant cannot go past when she throws.
- Measure to the first dent in the snow where the squash lands.
- The longest toss wins.

ROPE PULL

This event takes more than brute strength–it takes cunning!

- Build two platforms by rolling snow into a snowball as you would for building a snowman. When the snowball is at least 3 feet across, make an area to stand on by scraping the top of the snowball with a shovel until it is flat.
- Place the other snowball platform 10 feet away.
- For the event, have one participant stand on each snowball with one end of a rope in their hands.
- Now pull! The person left standing on the platform is the winner.

ROPE PULL

HULA TARGET

INNER TUBE RELAY

MORE! SNOW OLYMPICS

HULA TARGET

Hang a hula hoop from a tree or have a person hold it. The first participant throws snowballs at the hula hoop until he makes it through the center. The distance between the hoop and the players depends upon their skill level. The person with the fewest number of tosses needed to make it through the center of the hula hoop wins.

INNER TUBE RELAY

You will need at least a slight slope for this event, and one inner tube per team. Begin the relay with the teams at the top of the slope. At the blow of a whistle one person from each team (or a set of people) slides down the hill, and then runs back up to the top of the hill where the inner tube is passed on to the next person, or set of people. The team who completes the relay fastest receives the gold medal.

EXPLORE MORE!

Here are three ways to have more fun when you play hard outdoors in the winter:

* **DON'T OVERDRESS. This sounds funny, but most people dress too warmly when they are going outdoors in the winter for physical play. Exercise makes the body significantly warmer, and it is easy to overheat. Wear layers that you can peel off as you warm up.**

* **WEAR SOMETHING ON YOUR HEAD. The best way to keep your feet warm is to wear a hat! You lose a great deal of body heat through your head, which cools the body down.**

* **DRINK LOTS OF WATER. It is easy to forget to drink when you are outside, but it is important. In winter, the air you breathe in needs to be warmed and moistened, which can use more water from your body than when the weather is warm. And because you usually sweat under your clothes when playing hard outdoors, you can get dehydrated very easily. Drink up! It is nearly impossible to drink too much water.**

SNOWFLAKE CATCHER

Look for a used piece of clothing made of black velvet or velveteen in a thrift store, or check your local fabric store and see if they have scraps for sale. The raised nub in the black velvet holds the snowflake up and allows the cold air to circulate around it, keeping the flake intact longer. In a pinch, you can use any type of black fabric.

WHAT YOU WILL NEED:

piece of cardboard 5 by 6 inches

piece of black velvet or velveteen at least 6 by 7 inches

masking or duct tape

tongue depressor or large popsicle stick

magnifying glass

- To make your catcher, cut a piece of velvet large enough to cover and overlap the cardboard. Use the tape to secure the fabric tightly over the back of the cardboard, then tape one half of the tongue depressor to one end of the cardboard to create a handle.

- Place your snowflake catcher in the freezer until you are ready to use it—chilling the velvet assures the snowflakes won't melt on contact. Also, place the magnifying glass in the refrigerator so it won't fog up when you take it outside.

- During a snowstorm, take your catcher outdoors and allow the snowflakes to land on it. Study their unique beauty with the magnifying glass.

EXPLORE MORE!

There are seven basic kinds of snowflakes: Stellars and plates, which have the classic snowflake shape; columns and capped columns shaped just like their names; needles, which when you look closely, are long and have shaggy sides; spatial dendrites, which have tiny snowflake sprouts on top of the flake; and irregular crystals, which as their name implies, are irregularly shaped snowflakes.

The specific shape of a flake is determined by the temperature and how much humidity there is in the air as the flake falls. The more water there is high in the earth's atmosphere, the bigger the snowflake is. One of the largest snowflakes ever to reach earth was measured at more than 15 inches across! Snowflakes begin as ice crystals that can grow branches that collect more water, freeze, get heavy, and fall to the earth. And every snowflake is unique. In order to be identical, snowflakes would have to fall through the exact same conditions and even one molecule of water or a fractional difference in temperature can change their structure.

CHAIN GANG RACE

To win takes more than speed, it takes accommodation and cooperation. The closer you tie the players together, the harder it is. Do this race in the snow to make it even more difficult.

WHAT YOU WILL NEED:

as many people as you can gather

2 long ropes

- Divide into teams. Using the ropes, tie the players of each team together around their waists.
- Determine where the finish line will be and at "GO!" have each team race toward it. The first entire team across the finish line wins.

EXPLORE MORE!

Considered the halfway point between the winter solstice and spring equinox, Groundhog Day, February 2nd, is an old German tradition used to forecast the remaining winter weather. It was called Candlemas in the old days, and superstition held that if the weather on Candlemas was sunny enough to cast a shadow, the rest of the winter would be stormy and cold. If the weather was cloudy and cold, the rest of the winter would be fair and mild. The Germans used a badger's shadow, or no shadow, to foretell the winter weather on Candlemas. When the Germans came to America, they used a groundhog instead, and the day became known as Groundhog Day. But the groundhog's forecasting is not all that great. Records have been kept since the early 1900s, and the tradition has correctly predicted the weather only 39 percent of the time!

PINECONE FIRE STARTERS

Next time you are walking near evergreen trees, keep your eyes out for pinecones that have dropped to the ground. Collect them to make fire starters. They are lovely and make wonderful gifts when gathered together in a basket.

CAUTION: Hot wax can cause serious burns on your skin! Ask an adult to help you.

WHAT YOU WILL NEED:

beeswax (available at craft stores or candle making supply stores. You can use paraffin in a pinch, but the wax coating will not be as thick.)

cotton string or wick

pinecones

small can (a coffee can works great)

hammer and screwdriver

large pan

stove

newspapers

large bowl of ice water (optional)

- Place several chunks of beeswax in the small can (use a hammer and a screwdriver as a chisel to break the wax into chunks).
- Next, you will need to make a double boiler–the best way to melt wax because it uses water instead of direct heat.

THE DOUBLE BOILER:

- Pour several inches of water into the large pan, then lower the can with the wax into it.
- Place the pan on the stove and melt the wax over medium-high heat (it can take between 10 and 30 minutes).

- While you are waiting for the wax to melt, tie the string or wick around the pine cone, leaving several inches on one end of the string to use as a dipper. This will also serve as the wick. Once the wax is melted, let it cool for 10 minutes; cooling allows the wax to make a thick coat on the pine-cone.
- Dip the pinecone by the string into the wax once it has cooled. You may have to dip twice to get a thick enough coating of wax on the pinecone. To cool the wax quickly between dips, you can dunk the cone into the ice water after the first dip, then add another layer of wax.
- Lay the pinecone on the newspapers to cool. Repeat these steps with the other cones.

You can save the fire-starters in a zipper-type plastic bag until you are ready to use them. They will keep indefinitely if they do not get damp.

Because you have melted wax, why not make waterproof matches? Dip the heads of wooden matches into the wax and lay them on the newspapers until the wax has hardened. Store the matches in a zipper-type plastic bag too.

When ready to make a fire, place a teepee of kindling (small, skinny pieces of wood no bigger around than the size of your thumb) around the fire-starter and light the string. When the kindling is burning brightly, add larger chunks of wood to the fire.

EXPLORE MORE!

Many animals hibernate during the winter to survive the cold. Hibernation is a deep sleep that allows animals to conserve energy when food is scarce. Hibernating animals need very little energy to survive—their heart rates can drop to only 5 to 10 beats per minute, and they can breathe as little as once an hour. Most hibernating animals eat a lot of food before winter sets in. Their body stores the food as fat used to fuel bodily functions as they sleep.

ICE CANDLE HOLDER

This is a beautiful way to light the dark winter nights. If your weather is not cold enough to freeze these holders outdoors, use your freezer.

WHAT YOU WILL NEED:

nonstick cooking spray

plastic bucket

water

votive candle

- Spray the inside of the bucket with the cooking spray–to help slide the candle holder from the bucket.

- Fill the bucket with water and place outside when the temperature is below freezing.

- Leave overnight or until the water has frozen several inches thick on top. Water freezes in the bucket beginning on the edges, so along the inside and bottom of the bucket there will still be water under the ice. When you pour off this water, a space is created inside the ice to fit your candle.

- Next, slide the ice candle holder from the bucket. If it does not come easily, run warm water around the outside of the bucket for a couple of seconds.

- Drain off the water, then place the holder by itself outside or in your freezer for several hours.

- When it is dark, you can place the votive candle either inside the ice holder, or you can invert the holder over the candle.

EXPLORE MORE!

As the earth orbits the sun, it gradually tilts toward and then away from the sun causing our seasons. This tilt is the reason it is summer in the southern hemisphere of the world when it is winter in the northern hemisphere. You can watch the tilt of the earth in its orbit with this simple activity.

Buy a disposable panoramic camera and photograph the western horizon as the sun sets. Take your photos from a deck, porch, or sidewalk where you can mark the ground at the tip of your feet with masking or duct tape. Next, write the date and time you took the photo on a calendar. Once a month for several months take a photo of the horizon as the sun sets from the same place (feet on the tape). When you develop the film, match the photos with the negatives to put them in proper order. The number one negative is your first date and so on. Then use the calendar to date each photo with a marking pen. Line up the photos and compare. You will find that the sun sets more northerly as the spring draws nearer.

ICICLE ICE CREAM

Want to make ice cream in a hurry? This recipe is an easy one that uses either ice or icicles from outside.

WHAT YOU WILL NEED:

chocolate milk

enough ice or icicles to fill the bowl

salt

small jar or glass

aluminum foil

large plastic bowl

spoon for stirring

- Fill the jar two-thirds full of chocolate milk and cover with the foil.

- Place the jar in the center of the bowl and add a layer of icicle pieces around it.

- Sprinkle salt heavily over the ice. Add more layers of ice and salt until the ice reaches the top of the jar.

- Take the foil off the jar and begin to stir the chocolate milk. Stir until the chocolate milk starts to freeze (at least 15 minutes). When the mixture is the consistency of soft ice cream, it is ready to eat.

For an added treat, pour chocolate syrup over your ice cream and add a touch of whipped cream.

INDEX

WHO WE ARE

As long as I can remember, I have loved spending time outdoors. As a child in Idaho, my brothers, sisters, and I raced through wheat fields, played baseball, went fishing, and swam in irrigation ditches.

My husband of 25 years and I have four wonderful kids—a daughter and three sons. As they grew up, we took them skiing and hiking and biking. Today the kids earn money by fishing in Alaska over the summer, studying the roots of acacia trees in Costa Rica, and scuba diving to clean the bottoms of boats.

Over the years I have written for *Mothering Magazine*, *Reader's Digest*, and I have a story in *Chicken Soup for the Traveler's Soul*. My Mudpies column has appeared in regional parent magazines throughout the United States including magazines in New York, San Francisco, Atlanta, and Seattle. And this column inspired four books published by Tricycle Press: *The Mudpies Activity Book: Recipes for Invention*; *More Mudpies: 101 Alternatives to Television*; *Lotions, Potions, and Slime*; and *The Mudpies Book of Boredom Busters*.

Each summer our family lives and works in Alaska during Bristol Bay sockeye season—a dream life for someone like me. A large population of grizzly bears live near us and we pour plaster of paris in their mammoth tracks to take home. We live in a trailer and it feels every bit as comfortable as our big house in the Pacific Northwest.

NANCY BLAKEY

DANA DEAN DOERING

I love children! Throughout a 30-year career in pediatrics and child and adolescent psychiatric mental health, I have spanned the globe facilitating and photographing children's play. And I have found that play, especially play in and with nature, is essential and gives us a feel of the real world.

My own love of nature began when, at one, my favorite toys were jars of bugs and butterflies and later evolved into a lifestyle of scuba diving and shark photography in the far reaches of the Bay of Siam and St. Croix, USVI. My fondest memories are all outdoor moments—riding horseback through streambeds, crashing wildly through surf, wading in monsoon rains, and standing in the spray of waterfalls.

Teaching each other to play is our most important work. The most important place to do that work is outside. Currently I work and play in the Pacific Northwest.

AN INVITATION

As you spend time outdoors doing these activities, you may uncover new ideas or projects of your own. If you would like to share your discoveries and adventures, write to

Nancy Blakey c/o Tricycle Press, PO Box 7123, Berkeley, CA 94707-7123

Or log on to www.nancyblakey.com